ALSO BY MALCOLM BOSSE

The Vast Memory of Love
Mister Touch
Stranger at the Gate
Fire in Heaven
The Warlord
The Man Who Loved Zoos
The Incident at Naha
The Journey of Tao Kim Nam

FOR YOUNG ADULTS

Captives of Time
The Barracuda Gang
Ganesh
Cave Beyond Time
The 79 Squares

DEEP DREAM OF THE RAIN FOREST

DEEP DREAM

·OF THE·

RAIN FOREST

MALCOLM BOSSE

FARRAR, STRAUS AND GIROUX

NEW YORK

For Fender Bender, Giggs, the Keeks

Deeds cannot dream what dreams can do.
        —e. e. cummings

DEEP DREAM OF THE RAIN FOREST

· 1 ·

The longhouse was sleeping beside the broad, smooth, iron back of the river. It was the time of dreaming, a time welcomed by the Iban, who often found the meaning of their lives in the world of dreams. Mangy dogs and humpbacked pigs were growling and grunting in their sleep beneath the tall hardwood stilts of the dwelling. From beyond the first line of sago palms came the raucous sounds of the jungle, the crashing and snorting and shrieking that never awakened the Iban, who were accustomed to such nighttime noise. In their slumber, they merely snuffled at the ghostly cry of the winged beast called Pebnako, who was sometimes heard but never seen.

Two hundred men, women, and children slept in the row of forty cubicles that lined the veranda. From the ceiling hung a dozen baskets woven of rattan. They contained weathered skulls, the prized possessions of the Iban, who had been headhunters for generations. Such a "headhouse" was hanging in front of the room in which Bayang slept. Son of the longhouse's headman, Bayang had seen these hanging baskets all his life. Often they were the last thing he saw before falling into

3

a contented sleep. But tonight a dream unlike any other awakened him with a violent start, so that he sat bolt upright, gasping for breath.

Bayang did not fall asleep again but lay there filled with the dream until the first light appeared in the sky. Because the dream was so great, so strange, he wondered why a small brown stone hadn't appeared in his hand. No one in the longhouse had ever seen such a stone, but no one questioned its existence either, because people said if you have a dream that can change your life, a small brown stone will probably lie in your hand when you awake. None lay in his, but even so, Bayang knew without the slightest doubt that this dream would change his life.

When sunlight was coming through the trees, he saw his mother rise from her mat and leave the room for the veranda. There she'd build a fire to steam some yams and rice for the morning meal. There was now enough light for Bayang to see the designs of flowers on the tall ceramic jar that his mother had brought to the longhouse when she married his father. This Chinese jar had a dragon-shaped lid; nothing was kept in this treasured jar, allowing spirits to spend the night there if they wished.

The dream had been very great: of that Bayang was certain. No shaman was needed to tell someone when a dream was great. It lay within like a glowing egg, and when finally it hatched, the spirit of it joined with yours and you were someone new.

Bayang got up and went outside. The first thing he saw was the headhouse that hung directly in front of the family room. In the first rays of sun shining through the branches, he saw a wasp emerging from one of the heads in the rattan webbing. Then a few more large blue wasps trundled from the entrance,

4

which was the base of the skull where it had been severed from the spinal column many years ago by his grandfather, who had been a great warrior.

The boy smelled salt fish and pungent smoke and heard from the jungle a troop of gibbons whooping in the top branches of a camphor tree. He often wished for such long arms to swing him high above ground through the jungle.

Bayang was almost fully grown, slightly over five feet tall, with thick thighs and a muscular torso. His black hair was cut across his copper-colored forehead in a perfectly straight line (his mother saw to that) but in back was gathered into a long ponytail. From childhood he'd worn weights on his ears, so that now their lobes were distended into long loops. He wore a loincloth, and at his waist, on a rattan belt, dangled the scabbard containing a two-foot-long parang—the famed knife of Borneo. He already possessed a few tattoos: stars on his back, half-moons and palm leaves on his chest. They'd been made by hammering charcoal soot into his skin with a bamboo stick. The point was kept blunt to challenge the courage of a young warrior.

Walking down the veranda, past a line of women working over their fires and pots, he came to the notched pole, as slim as a man's arm, that served as a ladder. Bayang went down it standing straight up, placing his feet agilely in the small descending grooves until he reached the ground far below. Two boys his age were playing with a ball made of coconut leaves plaited together. When they asked him to join them, he shook his head and asked if they had seen Duck Foot. Frowning, they pointed toward the back of the longhouse.

Bayang found her there, feeding chickens that had been released from their nighttime cages. Duck Foot was younger than Bayang, with large, wide-set eyes and a pretty face. But there wasn't a single tattoo on her body, although Tambong—

5

for that was her real name—was a girl on the verge of woman-hood and therefore should have a number of tattoos already. The old crone who did the longhouse tattooing refused to touch the girl because of her bad foot. Tambong had been born with thin webs of skin between the toes of her left foot. Because of this deformity, people called her Duck Foot and none of the children played with her, except Bayang, who let no one choose his friends for him. Aside from feasts when everyone participated, Duck Foot stayed mostly by herself, a thoughtful, quiet girl who did her chores without complaint.

When Bayang spoke to her, she turned sharply from the chickens, surprised by the sound of her real name, until she saw that Bayang had spoken it. Then she smiled faintly.

Without hesitation he told her the dream. He had been swallowed by a big fish that swam farther than the gods could walk. Looking through the eyes of the fish, as if he'd been inside its body, Bayang had seen the entire world. It was so big that he hadn't seen to the end.

Bayang laid his hand out flat, parallel to the ground. "Green below." He thrust his hand high over his head. "Blue above. I saw it go that way without end. Then the Big Fish spit me out."

"May I ask?" The girl deferred to the young warrior.

"Ask."

"When he swallowed you, didn't you die?"

"I must have died then. But in his belly I lived again. And I crawled through him to his eyes and looked out at the world from his eyes."

Duck Foot looked at him curiously. "Then you died and came alive again. You are new," she murmured.

He shook his head. "No, I am not new yet. But if I follow the dream, I will be. After spitting me out, the fish said if I swim into his belly again, I will see the world even better. I will know what it is."

The girl couldn't meet his eyes, but glanced sidelong at him. "You will be a great man."

"Only if I swim into his belly again."

"May I ask?"

"Have I ever said you couldn't ask?"

"No."

"Ask."

"To swim again in the fish's belly, you must find him. Does it mean searching far and everywhere?"

After a thoughtful pause, Bayang nodded.

"In the dream world?"

"I believe the search must be in this world. The last thing the fish said was to watch the duck flying. When I awoke, I came looking for you. You are the duck flying."

When she said nothing, Bayang continued. The dream meant they must go together in search of the Big Fish. She must go with him—the duck, flying. And if they failed to find the Big Fish, the egg left in Bayang's soul by the dream would never hatch, but spoil there and make him heavy, slow, and tired; its rottenness would flow through his body until the ruined dream destroyed him. So together they must search through the world for the Big Fish so he could swim again in its belly. He repeated it. "Together."

She didn't look at him.

"Will you go with me, then?" Bayang asked sternly.

The girl stared at the ground. "I'm afraid."

"Will you go with me?"

Duck Foot had tears in her eyes as she looked directly at him. "Yes. I'll go. We have no choice, either of us. Such a great dream must be obeyed."

Bayang found his father in the rice padi. Although Pamancha Dana was headman of the longhouse, he worked in the fields alongside the other villagers. What distinguished him from the other men was his tattoos. Like his companions, he wore palm leaves and stars on his back and arms, but he alone had the design of hornbill birds on his legs. That set him apart as a chief. Only three other men in the longhouse wore, as Pamancha Dana did, the dots and cross-hatchings on the palm of his right hand, which signified that he had taken a head.

Many years ago the white man had ordered the Iban to stop their headhunting, and they had stopped it except for sudden encounters with other tribes in the jungle. Then, if someone died in a fight, his head was taken. It was only to be expected—as natural as storm clouds delivering rain. Pamancha Dana had taken a Kayan head before marriage. Proudly he'd presented it to his bride, who wrapped it in a blanket she'd woven. How the other women had envied her! In the old days a man could win a bride solely by presenting her with the gift of a head. Now it was rare for a bride to be given one. The Kayan head taken by Bayang's father was not kept in the rattan headhouse on the veranda but was stored in a corner of the family room, cherished like the Chinese jar and an old brass gong and Pamancha Dana's great-grandfather's headhunting sword.

Today Pamancha Dana and the other men were transplanting rice shoots in swampland burned off for padi. They poked holes with dibble sticks and pushed the shoots into the warm mud.

Seeing his son, Pamancha Dana stopped work and broke off a piece of tobacco from a stick of it. He began chewing this sugee while Bayang told him of the dream and what he intended to do.

"You've not come to me for permission?" Pamancha Dana demanded sharply.

"The dream has told me what to do, so I must do it."

"No matter what I say?"

The boy met his father's hard eyes. "I honor you, Father, but I must do what the dream says."

Pamancha Dana smiled. "Good. You understand the power of the dream. I agree with you it's a great dream. A god has put it in your head." Chewing the sugee methodically, the headman narrowed his eyes. "In the old days our people chose war chiefs only by what they dreamed, because such dreams gave the strength to attack. Now people think of them as something from the past. But what you have been given is such a dream right now, today, this moment as the sun rises over the tallest tree. If you fail the dream, you will die."

"I know that, Father."

"Good. You have listened to the dream. It is in your head and I see it shining from your eyes. Where will you look first for the Big Fish?"

"I don't know."

"Listen to me. This morning I heard a new riddle." Pamancha Dana loved riddles, as did most Iban. "Tell me, son, what are six posts trapped in a rock?"

Bayang thought a long time before attempting an answer. Then he said, "A turtle. Four posts are the legs. Another's the tail. The last post is the head. And everything is under a hard shell—a rock."

"Good. Three of us heard it, but none knew the answer. I think the dream is already working in you. You say the fish told you to follow the flying duck. That's your start. Follow it." The headman scowled. "But where will you find the duck?"

"Here in the village. It is Duck Foot."

"Duck Foot?" the headman repeated in astonishment.

"She goes with me. I will follow her."

"You will let a girl lead the way?" the headman asked incredulously. But after a long pause he added, "Yes. That must be. It's what the dream says. Duck Foot must show you the path to take." Reaching out, he gripped his son's arm. "I will tell you this now. Always I've felt you would do great things—lead a war party, take the head of an enemy, build a new longhouse, find better land for padi. Your dream tells me you will succeed or die. It's no dream of small things. I'm proud the dream is yours, even though you're too young for wandering in the jungle. Perhaps this dream has marked you for death. Yet the dream can't be dreamed and let go. I could not have a son of mine let it go and still call him my son. If you find the Big Fish and swim in its belly again, you'll know more than any of us have ever known. More than your fathers long dead ever knew. More than any great warrior, more than your grandfather or his father ever knew. You'll know the mysteries—or end your life trying. Either way, you will make me proud."

Next day his mother gave him hunks of salt fish wrapped in banana leaves along with pieces of wild pig that she had smoked in a section of bamboo. That was all. She took him by the shoulders and smelled his face affectionately, drawing her breath in deeply. She pronounced the names of gods in order to protect him. She never cried, though her lips trembled.

Bayang took up his dart quiver and blowgun, seven feet long, which was fitted with a sharp point near the tip so it could also be used as a spear. In a small pouch he kept a thick paste of poison made from the sap of ipoh trees.

Walking down the veranda to the door of Duck Foot's family, he noticed with distaste that their portion of the bamboo floor was unswept as usual, dirty from scraps of food. Not only did the girl have a bad foot, but her family was lazy and worthless as well. They were letting her go with him because she had no future in the village and he was a chief's son. When he called her name harshly, Duck Foot emerged, with the family staring curiously from behind her shoulder.

"May I ask?" Duck Foot said.

"Ask."

"How long will we be gone? They want to know."

"I don't know. Perhaps forever," he answered in a hard voice, meant to sound like that of a grown warrior, contemptuous of danger.

Then they set out, with people along the veranda watching them silently. Bayang wondered if they were thinking this was the last time they would ever see the headman's son and the crippled girl. He glared at them. When he and Duck Foot climbed down the ladder, a few boys giggled and hooted, but at a respectful distance.

Reaching the wall of surrounding jungle, Bayang halted. So did Duck Foot, waiting for him to choose a direction and set out.

"You go first," he ordered roughly.

When she failed to move, he said it again. "You go first. I will follow."

"May I ask?"

"Ask, and never ask me again if you may ask. From now on, ask."

"Why must I go first and you follow?"

"I must watch the duck flying."

After a long hesitation, Duck Foot stepped forward into the jungle. Walking with a limp, she glanced anxiously back at him.

"Go on," Bayang commanded. "Go on. Lead us away from here." Watching her footprints sink into the soft mud, he followed. Her prints to the left had the look of a duck's webbed foot. For an instant he wondered why he was allowing this outcast girl to lead him through the unknown jungle, but only for an instant, because the dream was at his ear, telling him that he must do what it told him to do.

· 2 ·

F ar to the southwest of the longhouse, on the Sarawak River
  near the coast of Borneo, lay the port of Kuching. Ships put
in there from the South China Sea. To Kuching's thriving mar-
ketplace came Malayan traders with goods from Singapore and
Chinese farmers with rubber and pepper raised on their upriver
plantations.

It was the year 1920, when the Brooke family, under British
protection, were rulers of the land called Sarawak, a land of
unexplored jungles and many tribes so isolated that they were
scarcely known to one another.

Harry Windsor, a tall, husky boy of fifteen, had been in
Kuching now for three months and was bored. He had visited
the museum and Chinese temples and had crossed the Sarawak
River to the old fort with its single cannon and through his
uncle had met the ruling Rajah, Charles Vyner Brooke, for
Tuesday tea in the colonial palace fronted by rolling lawns and
guarded by dark-skinned Dayak in British uniforms.

But Harry wanted to see more. He had heard of the headhunting Iban and Kayan and Penan and Kelabit tribes who

lived in houses as long as a cricket field and who killed game with poisoned darts and who, for nearly a century, had defied the white man's attempt to bring them under control. So for many days now, usually at dinner, Harry had pestered his Uncle Julian to take him on the next expedition inland.

Julian Windsor resisted, though he had deep affection and sympathy for this freckle-faced, red-haired nephew: affection, because Harry had an adventurous nature much like his own; and sympathy, because Harry was an orphan.

Harry's father, a captain in the British Expeditionary Force, had died in July 1918 during the Second Battle of the Marne. Then, in a bizarre tragedy, Harry's mother had been struck and killed in early 1919 by a military truck on a London street during the homecoming celebration of his father's own artillery unit. The lorry driver had been drunk.

Until then Harry had been a good student, but because of his grief he began to do poorly in school. The headmaster suggested to Harry's guardians, a distant cousin and her husband, that the boy take some time off. They readily agreed to let Harry accept his uncle's invitation to come East and stay awhile in Kuching. Julian Windsor was a state officer there; his chief task was to keep the peace in the outlying districts.

"I can't go back to school until the winter term," Harry pointed out, fork poised above a slice of beef. "I have enough time to go with you."

"True," Uncle Julian acknowledged.

"In the museum I looked at all the stuffed jungle animals and the human skull in a basket. I'd like to see the animals in the real jungle and one of those skulls hanging in a real long-house."

Uncle Julian pulled thoughtfully at his flaring sideburns and cleared his throat. "If you aren't careful, one of those skulls could be your own."

"I thought headhunting was outlawed."

"Indeed it is." Uncle Julian sighed. "But headhunting is in the Iban blood. In the old days, they tell me, the women went into frenzies of joy when a warrior brought home a head. Even today, given the chance, the Iban will take heads. But it's not only tribesmen you have to worry about out there." Uncle Julian waved his fork to indicate the land beyond the room. "There's the jungle itself. You haven't any idea what it is."

Harry shrugged. "Trees, bushes, animals."

"Heat. Heat that takes you by the throat and stops you dead in your tracks sometimes. It can render a strong man as weak as a puppy. And there're cobras fifteen feet long, man-eating crocs, nasty-tempered wild boars. And of course there's the fuzzy red caterpillar to give you trouble."

"Trouble?" Harry laughed. "A caterpillar?"

"There's not much to laugh about in the jungle, nephew. Step on one of those caterpillars, you'll have more trouble than you ever bargained for. Its tiny hairs enter your skin and cause sores that fester for months. And of course, there are other little matters. If your food's gone because your boat capsizes or monkeys steal it, you learn to live on fried lizard and bee larvae soup. If it sounds unappetizing, believe me, it is. Sometimes, because of thick branches overhead, you don't see the sun for days. Leaves with edges like knife blades slice into your hands and face. Leeches bloat themselves on your blood, though you don't know it till the end of the day's march, when you peel back your trouser legs and see them huge and wriggling, fat and content from feeding on your legs. That's the jungle, Harry." Satisfied that he'd frightened the boy, Uncle Julian added with a smile, "Frankly, I don't believe you're ready for it. And you haven't learned enough Iban."

Since arriving in Borneo, at his uncle's insistence Harry had taken daily lessons in the language. "You can't live here without knowing the native languages," his uncle had claimed, "especially Iban. Every Englishman who comes out here must learn."

Tonight Uncle Julian repeated it. "Yes, every Englishman, including you, my boy, must learn."

"You mean I'm not ready for the jungle because I don't know a language? That's like saying you can't see Rome until you know Latin."

His uncle glared at the insolence, but that didn't stop Harry, who put his knife and fork down hard on the plate. "Sir, I'm a Windsor. My great-grandfather lost a leg at Waterloo. My grandfather fought at Sevastopol in the Crimea. One great-uncle trekked across the Sahara. Another reached the Victoria Falls—full of disease, he died there. And you, Uncle, you were wounded at the Somme, or otherwise you might have gone down with my father at the Marne. All of you are what I come from. I don't want to live my life in pretty little ports like Kuching."

"So you say," Uncle Julian muttered gruffly. Furiously he cut off a slice of beef, but, lifting it to his lips, he sighed as if weary, put down his fork and slammed the table hard with his hand. "What in bloody hell can I do with a Windsor boy!" Again he sighed; this time it was accompanied by a faint smile. "Well, the Iban have their bloodlust. I suppose we Windsors are entitled to our own. You really do want to see what it's like out there?"

"Yes, sir," Harry said eagerly.

"Then so you shall." Julian's smile turned to a sad frown. "There's no one out here I must answer to for my conduct and judgment concerning you, Harry. I'll have to live with it."

"Does that mean you'll take me on the next show?"

Julian smiled at the boy's use of military slang. "But don't get your hopes up. It won't be the sort of adventure you expect. Merely a routine expedition."

"When? Where are we going?"

"In about a week. First by sea along the coast to check on some port towns. Then inland to the tribes."

Harry's eyes were shining. "To see if there's trouble?"

"Listen here, my boy, don't start by expecting trouble. Anyway, there haven't been war parties out for a long time. The tribes are calm. Don't look so bloody disappointed!" Julian told his nephew with a guffaw. "Things can go horribly wrong in a moment out there. You might have your trouble yet."

Harry smiled.

Harry Windsor was not as confident as he seemed. But he knew his uncle would never take along someone timid and unsure. All his life, Harry had dealt with hard-bitten men like his uncle and like his father, who had been a member of an Arctic expedition before the war. From stern masters in school Harry had learned the harsh realities of life. With his mother's consent (she was an admiral's daughter), his father had sent Harry to schools renowned for building character. That meant thrashings with a cane. That meant absolute silence in the classroom. That meant getting up before sunrise and washing your face in water so cold there were filaments of ice at the edge of the old ceramic bowls that had been used by students for generations. That meant brutal ragging from the senior boys and standing up to them when challenged. Lucky for Harry he'd been strong. He knew how to stand up. Those chilly years in damp old buildings of stone had taught him how.

But the truth was Harry felt homesick. He loved the rocky, fog-heavy coasts and rolling green countryside of England. In school he had memorized these lines from Shakespeare, lines that meant a great deal to him:

DEEP DREAM OF THE RAIN FOREST

. . . this little world,
This precious stone set in the silver sea . . .
This blessed plot, this earth, this realm, this England . . .

Yet what Uncle Julian said was also true: adventuring was in the Windsor blood. Pushed forward into each Windsor life by a deep impulse of curiosity was the desire to encounter the unknown. He could no more deny this in himself than hold back the dawn. So the week of waiting to leave Kuching was a torment. He imagined it must have been the same for all the Windsors as they waited to go into battle or to set out for uncharted territory.

By paddle steamer, Julian Windsor (his title was Senior Enforcement Officer, Sarawak Protectorate) and twenty men—five of them native Land Dayak and fifteen Britons—along with an English boy of fifteen, headed slowly eastward along the northern coast of Borneo.

They stopped at port towns long enough for Officer Windsor to consult with the local official, usually a Malay, and inspect the warehouse area for evidence of smuggling. Allowed by his uncle to go ashore, Harry wandered along the rows of dirty little shops where Chinese merchants sold medicines such as fermented octopus in jars or black cotton shirts for men and gownlike cheongsams for women. There were many loafers around the wharves; they sat on bales, smoking and watching cargo ships enter port and await their turn at the docks. Flat-hulled sailing vessels, often used by pirates, swung at anchor farther out.

The weathered shacks, the whine of boat winches, the shouting in half a dozen dialects of Chinese and in Malay and Dayak and broken English, the stinking mud churned by stevedores, the gray scum made by engine exhausts and by oil

17

spilled along the shorelines of river towns—all of this motion and sound and smell appealed immensely to Harry Windsor. It meant that he was moving farther from the world he had known.

His excitement showed on his face. Once when he was standing on the paddle steamer's deck, observing some gulls swoop over a stack of crates, his uncle came up alongside him and said, with a rueful laugh, "What in bloody hell out there makes you look so happy?"

Harry merely smiled. He knew that Uncle Julian knew without asking.

In Miri they hired three trackers for the journey inland, then proceeded by motorized dugout canoe to a riverside village called Pangkalan Lubang, where at low tide they had to climb a notched pole from boat to riverbank. All the natives casually walked straight up the eight-foot ladder as if it were horizontal instead of vertical. A few of the Englishmen, including Officer Windsor, did, too, but most had to climb it like shinnying up a tree. Finally it was Harry's turn. He looked at the men lining the bank above him, then at his uncle's grinning whiskered face, and their anticipation of his awkwardness made him determined to walk the slim pole upright. Once he placed his foot into the first narrow notch, however, he knew it was impossible. One step upward and he would surely pitch off balance into the river. So, like many of the others, he climbed up ignominiously with both arms wrapped around the pole. When he reached the bank, his uncle gave him a swift but approving nod. He hadn't been foolhardy. He had done the right thing.

Nomadic Penan tribesmen were reported in the area, so Officer Windsor wanted to meet and talk with them. A tracker was dispatched to find out where they were. Meanwhile, the expedition pitched tents outside the village and bedded down to wait.

Next day the Penan had still not been located, so Officer Windsor used the opportunity to take his nephew for a visit to a neighborhood cave. "The Niah Cave," he explained to Harry, "is one of the largest in the world—and one of the strangest."

"Why?"

"Because of the swiftlets. They're tiny birds that dart so fast you can hardly see them in flight. They build nests on the cave roof by gluing bits of leafy twig together with their spit. This spit is highly prized by Chinese cooks, who make a very expensive soup from it."

"From spit?" Harry screwed up his freckled face.

"I don't think you're too impressed by the idea of Niah Cave."

Out of politeness Harry said, "I haven't seen it yet, so I don't know."

"That's right. Don't pass judgment on Niah until you see it. For that matter, it's best not to pass judgment on anything about the jungle until you've been there."

It occurred to Harry that although his uncle was a Windsor, he wasn't rash at all but cautious. Harry had always felt a little ashamed of his own tendency to be cautious about things, because it seemed to him that his ancestors had all been hell-bent, impetuous, ready to plunge into danger at any moment. But perhaps it wasn't true. At least his uncle seemed to think and consider before he acted. Harry felt more comfortable now with his own nature, which was to do the same.

From the village of Pangkalan Lubang there was a short trek down a swampy path that ended, abruptly, at the yawning mouth of an enormous cave.

"Forty thousand years ago, Harry, men lived here in Niah

Cave," said Julian Windsor. He strode inside. Harry followed through the large entrance, taking no more than a few steps before the cool air surrounded him, along with a powerfully acrid stench. "Whew," he gasped. "That smell . . ."

"It's guano," his uncle explained. "A mixture of swiftlet and bat excrement. They sell it on the coast for fertilizer. Look up there." Julian was pointing to a long bamboo pole, its sections fastened together with pegs, running from cave floor to ceiling. The pole was so tall that Harry strained to see the end of it in the gloom of the cave. The bamboo swayed, and when it did, Harry saw something whitish and large moving along the roof among some short poles like a spider in its web.

"That's a man up there," Julian said. "He's a bird's nest gatherer who shinnies up the pole hand over hand. What he does is scrape the nests out of crevices in the roof." Pointing straight ahead into the blackness, he went on, "His partner is standing in a ravine right below the nests being scraped loose. When a nest falls, he locates it by the sound of it hitting the rocks. He doesn't use a light, just his ears. Believe me, it's not a very loud sound—after all, it's the sound of a small bunch of twigs. I have never heard it once, but I've seen these men rush up and find a fallen nest in the darkness as if they had a flashlight shining on it. When they get a bagful, they sell it to Chinese merchants, who market the nests to exporters who take the stuff to Hong Kong, Shanghai, Singapore. What the gatherer up there in the cave risks his life for ends up as expensive soup at a banquet." Julian squinted at his watch in the gloom. "We've come at the right time, Harry. It won't be long now. Just sit and wait."

They sat on a slippery rock and waited. His uncle said nothing, so Harry said nothing either, though he wanted to complain about the horrible smell. How could a man endure it hour after hour? Not to speak of climbing such a long, slim pole and leaning away from it and feeling around in search of twigs held together by bird spit? But Harry held his tongue; clearly, his uncle wanted the suspense to build up in silence. Uncle Julian wanted him to be surprised.

And he was.

In late afternoon, after watching the nest gatherers descend with the alacrity of monkeys, Harry noticed at the entrance of the cave a few flickering dots appear, then a few more. Finally—it seemed out of nowhere—a tremendous darting of tiny objects jittered in front of his eyes. Streams of them poured into the cave, as if a giant hand had shaken huge sackfuls of dust at the entrance. There was a sudden noise, which Harry realized after a moment was a twittering sound made by living things. Then he discerned the movement of countless little wings—birds, the swiftlets! They were flying into the cave, hundreds, thousands, so thick in their flight that Harry couldn't see the hill fronting the cave anymore; the green slopes had become a moving mass of black lines—the wings of swiftlets. He couldn't believe their numbers might increase, yet they did: at least two or three hundred little birds were flying over his head each time he took a single breath.

Another sound added to the shrill chirping of the swiftlets. This was a rustling, clacking, metallic sound that grew louder as the swiftlets entered the cave.

"Guess what that is," his uncle asked.

"I never heard a sound like that before."

"I'm sure you haven't. It's the sound of bats airing out their wings, preparing to fly. You see, my boy, up there in the crevices are not only swiftlet nests but a couple of million bats hanging upside down from the roof. The birds' day is the bats' night. Now the bats are getting ready for their own hunt."

"You mean, when the birds come into the cave, the bats go out?"

"The pattern never varies. The transfer happens simultaneously."

"How do they time it—going in and out at the same time?"

"Who knows? And they never collide. Millions of bodies hurtling through the air, but they never crash into one another. I have never heard of it happening. Now watch."

As his uncle had been talking, Harry saw overhead, coming from deep within the cave, a clattering mass of dark shapes funneling toward the entrance: bats, numberless, swarming. Soon the bats and swiftlets were passing, one group bound for a night's foraging and the other nestling down for a night's sleep.

"They're not all that inhabit this cave." Julian was staring back into the darkness. "You have snakes in there, and spiders, and centipedes eight inches long—poisonous to boot—and a dozen varieties of moth, some with the wingspan of a man's forearm, and a lot of lizards, and cockroaches bigger than the palm of your hand, and cave crickets large enough to crack open and devour the eggs of birds."

Harry stared into the darkness that seemed empty; now he understood it was teeming with life. "The men forty thousand years ago: I wonder what they thought of all this."

"Maybe what we do. Disbelief. Wonder. Awe."

"Yes, sir, that's what I feel."

That night they slept again near the village, which lay at the edge of the Bornean jungle. Beyond the tent wall, Harry could hear the night sounds: a dog barking, lizards cheeping, monkeys blaring from treetops, a bullfrog bellowing rhythmically in a nearby swamp. Without the interference of man-made noise, jungle sounds were absolutely clear, each distinct from the others. Far from being secretive and mysterious, these sounds were brash, purposeful, chatty. It was like a hundred conversations being carried on at once, but of course, Harry realized, he didn't know a single language being spoken. Even so, he might learn. Lying awake, eyes wide open, Harry felt that the world beyond his tent was less to be feared than to be understood. Perhaps he had seen the best of it already. Nothing out there beyond the tent could be as wild and beautiful and awesome as what he had seen in the cave today. Wasn't it true? He fell asleep on that question.

Next morning, as they ate rice and wild vegetables gathered by the Dayak guides, Officer Windsor turned to his nephew and said, "Am I right that the cave impressed you?"

"Yes, sir. I never saw anything like it. I don't think anything could ever equal it."

"Think you've seen the best first?"

It was what Harry had wondered last night, but he kept the idea to himself.

"It's bad form to make definitive judgments out here, my boy," his uncle said after a long silence. "Almost always you're proved wrong. What happened yesterday was this: you saw something unusual. Bully for you, but that's all it was. Today could be somewhat different. You might feel more than see. I mean feel in your mouth and ears, your heart and bones. Feel without thinking. At the end of the day you could quite possibly know more about yourself than you ever have. Not in your mind but in your body. In a sense, feel more body than you ever knew was there."

Harry was impatient with his uncle's lecture; he didn't understand it, but, more important, it didn't tell him what he wanted to know. "What happens today?" he asked.

"If the Penan haven't been located by noon—and I suspect they won't be—we'll head into the jungle and go looking for them. Today you just might see the jungle for the first time."

· 3 ·

They were traveling northward now; they would have described themselves as going toward the Batang and Baleh Rivers, because the Iban defined directions by the junction of rivers and streams. Duck Foot still led the way. She had become accustomed to it, although at first it had frightened and embarrassed her to lead the son of a headman. Now she merely went forward, with him silently behind her, listening to the sound of birds. As a young warrior, he'd been trained to interpret these sounds. So far, at least to her knowledge, nothing heard by him had told Bayang what to do. They simply went forward, awaiting a sign—perhaps from a birdcall, perhaps from a dream. Last night, to encourage dreaming, Bayang had slept on a hilltop where spirits like to stay, but this procedure, called nampok, had not worked. Although Bayang had called out to the spirits before sleeping, pleading with them to enter his dreams, none came in the dream hours to give him instructions or advice. All the travelers could do was keep moving until a sign told them otherwise. Even though they were meandering along, Duck Foot felt elated; the farther they went into the jungle, the more excited and hopeful she became. The Iban had always believed in the Bejelai, the Dream Walk, because such an adventure often changed the lives of people. And she was taking the Dream Walk with someone she was learning to trust.

For one thing, she was encouraged by Bayang's respect for the spirits. Each time he came to a river or stream, Bayang knelt beside the bank, drew his parang, and with its long blade cut the surface of the water, thus honoring the spirits of that neighborhood. Moreover, he hadn't left home without protection: around his neck hung two strands of lizard skin with jeemats attached to them—amulets of shell containing bits of owl bone and crushed insects. Iban who went to live in cities usually discarded such charms, calling them outdated, but Bayang kept with the old ways. Duck Foot liked that in him because she, too, believed in the old ways. Life had prepared her to do so.

Other children had always avoided her; if you were born with something wrong, it meant the spirits disapproved of you. Often, from loneliness, she crawled under the small meditation house used by the dayung, the village spirit man, to discuss magic and omens with visiting dayungs. Under there in the shadows, she heard through the floor slats what dayungs had to say about demons, journeys of the soul, the Land of the Dead, and the behavior of gods. Probably she knew more about the spirit world than anyone in the longhouse aside from the dayung and a few old people.

Convinced by Bayang's dream that his was a very important journey, Duck Foot hoped that by helping him search for the Big Fish and find his destiny, she might benefit her own life.

She had always harbored a wish to have tattoos like those of the other women in the longhouse. While limping along through the dense undergrowth, Duck Foot once again indulged her fantasy about having tattoos—denied her thus far because of her deformity. Unlike some girls, who feared the pain, she'd have both arms and legs, hands and feet, completely tattooed. The main design would be of a dragon with two heads or two dragons sharing one head. She'd have human shapes covering her lower legs; moons and triangles on her arms, except from elbow to wrist on the inside, which must be left bare. She'd have her toes done black and the knuckles of her hands swathed in nets of black lines. She'd cover as much of her skin as tradition allowed, ignoring the four years of pain that it would take for the artist to complete so many designs. She'd endure the numerous infections caused by soot being pounded into her flesh with bamboo needles. None of that mattered—not the pain or the festering sores or the taboo against eating certain foods while the tattooing progressed. Ultimately she'd be covered with dense blue-black patterns of great beauty. If she could someday have the honor of being tattooed, she'd not allow the artist's assistant to hold her down when the pain was terrible; to prove her courage, she'd order the assistant to stand back. Holding the washcloth herself, she'd calmly remove every trace of blood oozing from the blackened needle holes.

Hers would be a complete set of batek, designs on her body worthy of any Iban woman. Her own mother was shiftless and her father drank too much palm wine every night, but in the past there had been warriors in her family—heads they had taken now hung in a basket on the veranda. She wanted to emulate her ancestors, make their spirits proud of her by possessing a fine set of batek on her flesh. Duck Foot was sure that when they died, those ancestors had not been thrown off the bridge at the River of the Dead as many people were; by taking heads, they'd won the right to cross without interference from the guardians of the river. Though she'd been too young to see her eldest uncle when he lived, she knew that during festivals he had worn feathers of the hornbill in his hair—the mark of an honored headhunter. She was proud of her ancestors and wanted them to be proud of her.

Glancing back at Bayang, she regarded with approval his quiver of darts, his seven-foot blowgun, the anak parang (child-sized knife) and the two-foot parang, both in hardwood sheaths, attached to his rattan belt. Though young and not yet fully grown, he had the look of a true warrior. She felt that with Bayang her life might change. He had tattoos on his back and chest and a dream in his heart. If anyone could help her achieve her own dream, perhaps Bayang could. She'd follow him on his soul's journey to the end of the earth, though at the moment he was following her.

When he saw the group of folded leaves in the crotch of a small tree, Bayang halted. Up there was a nest of kessa ants. He didn't need to call out to Duck Foot. Hearing him stop, she turned instantly and followed his gaze upward. Without a word being exchanged, she gathered some wood and with her own anak parang began shaving off slivers for tinder. Bayang cut a foot-long section from a bamboo tree nearby, then found a piece of flint in his knapsack. Holding some of the tinder and the flint together, he struck it all hard against the bamboo. Sparks flew. The tinder smoked, glowed, flamed up; then he placed it in a handful of bark that Duck Foot had collected. A few more wood shavings were added before the fire caught enough for Duck Foot to place on top of it some pieces of wood. She built the fire while Bayang shinnied up the tree, parang drawn, and cut down the kessa nest. Although ants swarmed over the cluster of envelope-like leaves, Duck Foot lifted the fallen nest with both hands and threw it into the fire. Swiftly the ants burned off. Then after the folded leaves had lain on the fire for a while, Duck Foot dragged them off with a stick. When they'd cooled, she opened each one, exposing dozens of ant larvae, slightly smoked. Duck Foot waited respectfully for Bayang to reach in and pick up the first grubs. After he'd shoved them in his mouth, she took some for herself. They were delicious: warm, smoky, a little sour. They were especially good because the prepared food the two had brought along had run out that morning.

Bayang smiled and noted that although she wished to keep her look severe, Duck Foot smiled faintly back. He was pleased with her. She had a feel for the jungle, and just as she had worked silently and efficiently to prepare the kessa grubs, throughout the journey, at least so far, she had done her part. He had not altogether expected it. Like most of the others in the longhouse, he'd always felt the webbed foot made her less capable than other people. But if the spirits had disapproved of her at birth, perhaps later on they'd changed their minds. She had been chosen by them to lead the way in his Dream Walk. Even so, he wasn't sure yet of confiding all his thoughts to any girl.

For example, Bayang hadn't told her about the bad omen he'd noticed this morning when they set out. A white-headed hawk had crossed their path from left to right instead of right to left. It was not a particularly bad omen—others were much worse—but coupled with what happened yesterday, it meant difficulty on the trail. Yesterday he'd heard the cry of the wood-pecker, kotok. If the little yellow-and-red bird had called out *keing keing,* things would go well. But what Bayang heard was *tok tok tok,* the bird's inauspicious call. Perhaps a spirit out there was warning Bayang through the sound made by a woodpecker: it was how spirits often told men things. But thus far Bayang had no idea what the warning might be, and so instead of telling the girl, whom he didn't yet fully trust, Bayang kept it to himself.

Having eaten their fill of grubs, they continued their journey, with Duck Foot once again leading the way. They moved steadily if slowly through the lush undergrowth of the rain forest. They paid little attention to its rampant beauty—orchids and moonflowers and oleanders and bougainvilleas were everywhere—but concentrated instead on finding signs that might help them with their task. Suddenly Bayang found one. It took his sharp eye to notice that lying on the ground was something more than a short length of bamboo. Carved lightly into its side was the crude image of an owl. This was the work of Kayan. Once again he kept it to himself, watching the girl limp along ahead of him, the ankle above her webbed foot bobbing rhythmically, a stone charm tied to it.

The piece of bamboo was a bird-calling device. The Kayan were expert at using it to decoy owls. A Kayan blew into the tube of bamboo, one hand covering the far end. The hand was lifted away when about half the note was completed; the sound duplicated that of a certain owl. Hearing this familiar note, an owl would often fly close enough for a Kayan to shoot it down. Only the Kayan knew how to do this. There was no doubt in Bayang's mind that Kayan were in the neighborhood—the slick surface of the bamboo, without a speck of dust or dirt on it, its sheen immaculate, told him that it must have been dropped here within the last day.

So the Kayan, a traditional enemy, who would love to have his head and that of the girl, were quite possibly within calling distance. He was considering the idea of telling her now, because of the imminent danger, when from ahead of him Bayang heard the girl's sharp cry of Iban surprise: "Akai!"

Joining her, he saw what had caused the outburst: two sticks about four feet long were stuck at a slant into the ground. Notches on them were decorated with leaves and twigs. "Penan," he said.

"I thought it was Kayan," said the girl with a frown.

"No, it's Penan." Like other boys in the longhouse, he'd been taught Penan, Kelabit, and Kayan. Though he understood the language, he'd seen the Penan only once. They had fair skin, hated sunlight, lived deep in the forest. Although they made the finest blowguns of all the Dayak peoples of Borneo, they never killed animals they raised, such as pigs and chickens. They never sought or took heads, but remained averse to war and avoided it at all costs. They were despised by the warlike Kayan and Kelabit, but not by the Iban, who though warlike, too, respected the hunting skills of these strange and timid people. Bending closer to study the notched words, Bayang said them aloud slowly. "Hunt pig this way"—with the sign of an arrow pointing westward. So a hunting party had left a message for other Penan in the area. But there was also a message on the other stick: "White ghosts this way"—an arrow pointing northeast.

Looking up from the message sticks at the girl, who said nothing but eagerly awaited word from him, Bayang said, "There are strangers in the forest. White men."

The girl nodded somberly.

Encouraged by her restraint, Bayang said, "We'll stay here tonight, though Kayan may be nearby." Again he awaited her reaction, but there was none. She would not interfere with his decisions. "We'll stay and hope for a dream that'll tell us what to do." He added thoughtfully, "Or perhaps we'll have a sign."

Duck Foot no longer asked him if she could ask. She simply asked. "What can a sign tell us?"

"If we should search for the strangers."

"Why search for them?"

"I don't know," Bayang confessed. "Perhaps they'll lead us to the Big Fish."

"I understand. Tonight we sleep here," the girl said.

That night, while Bayang slept, Duck Foot remained awake, and for hours she watched the wheeling stars appear and disappear in a gap between branches. She thought of the work of demons, how they can be as tiny as gnats or look human; how they cause miscarriages in women and confuse men so they become lost in the jungle. She thought of her cousin who had died in childbirth. The dayung thrust thorns into the dead woman's feet to keep her from getting up and seeking revenge against her husband for giving her such bad luck. All sorts of strange ideas drifted through Duck Foot's mind like fireflies. Kayan she feared less than the antu buyo; and for the first time during the journey Duck Foot felt a wave of fear wash over her, so that only toward morning could she get a little sleep.

When he awakened, Bayang confessed sadly that nothing of importance had occurred during his sleep. In silence they ate some berries, then set out. But they had not moved a hundred yards away from the Penan message sticks before "Akai!" rang out again. This time the exclamation came from Bayang. He'd heard a long series of sounds coursing through the dawn light—*check check check!*—high-pitched, harsh, and rapid, followed by a low and throaty *jree*. It was the call of the crested jay. There were few more auspicious calls in the jungle. He glanced rapidly around and saw the jay. It had a dull brown back and gray underparts, but when it sat on the limb high over Bayang's head it showed a long, brilliantly blue tail.

Surely this jay had just carried a message from the spirit world. Bayang smiled gratefully up at the bird. Turning, he said to Duck Foot, "There was no dream, but I have a sign now. It says to find the strangers."

"If we find them, will they help us?"

Bayang shrugged. For the first time he felt a little impatient with the girl. Her question was not that of a warrior. But he replied like one. Gruffly he told her, "When my father explained omens to me, he warned me not to think too far ahead. Only a dayung can do that because he talks directly to spirits. It's enough for a warrior to have a sign that says where to go, what to do. Now we need only travel."

Stepping in front of her, Bayang took the lead.

Smiling behind his back, Duck Foot felt relieved. She was indeed taking the Dream Walk with someone she could trust.

· 4 ·

The Penan nomads were not found in the vicinity of the riverside village of Pangkalan Lubang; as Officer Windsor had explained to his nephew, the expedition would search for them, though with little chance of finding such elusive people. But surely a trek into the interior would let the government know what was happening to the tribes there.

"Something might well be wrong," Uncle Julian told Harry. "The Penan wouldn't have ventured this close to a village unless they wanted to barter, say, wax and wild rubber and snake venom for tobacco and salt. If they left without doing business, something must have alarmed them and sent them back into the deep jungle. And don't smile like that."

Harry couldn't help it. The waiting was over; that noon twenty-four men and a boy set out from Pangkalan Lubang.

First they had to cross a mangrove swamp. Many of the trees stood forty feet high. There were nibong palms, their slender stems crowned with tufts of drooping fronds. The wood was used for making darts for blowguns. Abik, an Iban tracker, told Harry this. Since leaving the coast, Abik had taken him under his wing, amused and perhaps touched by the young English-man's ignorance of the country. He pointed out the nipa, its trunk hidden by thick leaves that were used in making baskets and roofing for huts. He showed Harry the sago tree, from whose trunks starchy flour was made. Penan lived on sago much of the time, he noted contemptuously; it was not food for warriors. The bark of the tengah mangrove, after being boiled and crushed, he told Harry, was durable enough to make sails. To such explanations Harry listened as if sitting in the class-room of a demanding schoolmaster. His respectful attention was what finally kept him going, because at times, in panic, he wanted to escape the horror of the swamp and return to the safety of the village. Nothing could have prepared him for such a challenge. Aerial roots, high above the ground, spread out in a network of spidery fibers; some of them possessed thorns that ripped into Harry's shoulders and arms. Other roots de-ployed like the ganglia of a monster, tangles of them massed around tree trunks, with leaves so tightly packed that the space below was cast into deep shadow. Within that shadow were swarms of buzzing insects, most of them scrappy mosquitoes that gave Harry not one moment of rest. Sometimes he wanted to scream from the maddening harassment, yet Abik's response to them, a mild if steady brushing of his left hand across his face, humbled and calmed Harry enough to keep him going in silence. The heat and humidity took his breath away. Uncle had been right about the heat; there was nothing comparable to it in Harry's experience. It was like a fire sucking up the sur-rounding oxygen; it had him gasping, a powerful boy of fif-teen, while Abik and the other natives trudged blandly along. Even the British troops, experienced in such terrain, took the march stoically.

Until today Harry had liked his uncle, but without reason to admire him for something specific. That changed now, when

Harry observed Officer Windsor near the head of the column, slashing mangrove branches with his own parang like an Iban tracker, making a path forward through the muck, which stank hotly and wetly from decomposing fronds, rotting fruit, the tiny corpses of insects and lizards. In his pith helmet, sweating at his work, Uncle Julian had the look of an explorer, and this, too, sustained Harry—the idea of traveling with such a man into adventure. After two hours of marching, Harry had settled down, accepting the heat and fatigue, allowing curiosity to take the place of discomfort in his mind. When finally they emerged into a plain called a keranga, sparsely covered by shrubs and intermittent clumps of tall trees, Harry was almost sorry to leave the hot monotony and fierce tangle and oppressive smell of the mangrove swamp.

Before nightfall they pitched tents in the keranga near the edge of a dense growth of rain forest. There was a raucous whooping sound from the wall of foliage. Startled, Harry turned to look at the dusky stand of trees from where he sat on a boulder. Abik squatted nearby, smoking a cheroot, its tobacco wrapped in nipa leaf he'd collected that afternoon. Abik said in accented but understandable English, "Monkey make sound. Gibbon monkey." He made a funny face and swung his arms and imitated the whooping noise. Abik was small but wiry, his face as wrinkled as old leather, but his tattooed arms and thighs were powerfully muscled. "Tomorrow might see hornbill. Tonight see snake." He pointed at a tree beyond the boulder. Squinting, Harry saw a brownish snake, perhaps three feet long, draped motionless over a high branch.

"Snake fly," Abik said, grinning.

"Sure," Harry replied, returning the grin with his own. Abik was teaching him many words in Iban as they went along, but the fellow wasn't altogether trustworthy. A snake that could fly? I wasn't born yesterday, Harry told himself.

.

Next morning, while they were sitting around campfires, drinking coffee and eating canned beans and smoked beef for breakfast, Harry was facing the tree where the snake had spent the night. There it was, looking like a piece of brown rope. Apparently it hadn't moved an inch. Then abruptly, while Harry chewed a rock-hard piece of meat, he saw the snake rouse itself on the branch, slide off it, and improbably glide perhaps thirty or forty feet at an oblique angle downward into another tree, as gracefully as a hawk.

Abik chortled and slapped his knee at the awestruck look on the boy's face. "Fly! Sure! Wait today. Maybe see cobra. Some cobra big." Putting down his tin plate, Abik walked off a dozen paces. "That big." Curving his fore- and middle fingers, he struck down with them as if they were fangs. "Cobra do that, you die." He laughed again at the look on Harry's face.

Later that day, after a march through dense rain forest, the expedition stopped for a rest. Harry went to his uncle and asked about the flying snake. He was nervous about asking; what if Abik had tricked him into believing the creature was a snake? After all, out here nothing was as it seemed.

But his uncle confirmed it. "That's the paradise snake," he said. "It draws its belly in to make a groove like this." His uncle placed his palms together and opened them outward. "The groove makes a small sail along the length of the snake's body, so it can launch itself and glide down to lower limbs in another tree. I've seen them go fifty feet or more." Julian wiped sweat from his face with a kerchief, then smiled. "Think that's the strangest thing in the jungle, do you?"

"I don't know about that, sir. I'll wait and see."

"Spoken like a tracker."

In fact, Harry saw nothing during the next few days as strange as the paradise snake gliding through the air. But he saw his first hornbill—or, rather, heard it first before seeing it. The hornbill's wings flapped like heavy sheets made of leather as it plunged down into a tree overhead, shaking leaves off the branches. Its neck was bright orange, its prominent beak the color of ivory with a block of yellow-and-red cartilage mounted on top of it. The hornbill made a series of powerful hoots—a sound like wood creaking loudly—that *cack-cack-cacked* across the topmost limbs of the trees.

"Iban eat hornbill," Abik explained proudly. "Kayan never eat. They think hornbill is god. We think is good meat." Abik smiled broadly at what he seemed to think was a witty remark. "But we not wear hornbill feather without taking head. Take head, then wear hornbill feather." He said it so matter-of-factly that the subject might have been the weather.

Harry was learning to accept Abik for what he was—someone as unpredictable as the jungle itself.

Surely nothing was predictable here. When Harry heard a crashing overhead, then another some distance away, he didn't see anything. It was as if the sound existed without cause. Then suddenly through the foliage he saw a brown body—or was it a shirt? He couldn't be sure if a man was climbing a tree. Then swinging into focus was a long orange nose, bigger than a banana, and a rusty-colored head, and he was looking at a proboscis monkey. A leaf moved; it was a butterfly. A twig moved; it was a praying mantis. The jungle seemed silent and motionless, until he sat quietly and observed it. Then it became noisy, tumultuous. Animals had no respect for their neighbors. Even monitor lizards crashed through the undergrowth like runaway freight trains. And it didn't require animals to make the jungle sound alive. By his own actions Harry could cause his surroundings to come to life. For example, he took a noise in the undergrowth for something made by scurrying creatures; then he discovered that *he* was making the sound—his foot was pressing on a long root and the touch traveled perhaps a dozen feet away and rustled some dead leaves. Often he heard a sound like the quitting-time whistle of a Liverpool factory: a kind of high-pitched shriek. But here the sound was made by beetles, countless numbers of them, unseen in the burrowing darkness.

Roots made walking as difficult for Harry as if he were a toddler just learning how. His feet got tangled in them, and often from behind, after he'd stumbled and fallen, he heard Abik's suppressed giggle. But that was all right, Harry told himself, because he would learn. He was determined to win his uncle's approval, but more important, that of the Iban tracker who spoke six languages and bet money with other trackers on how many times a birdcall would be repeated. Abik told Harry about the old days when his grandfather was a coastal pirate with the Malays. When they fell upon a ship, the Malays took what plunder was there, but his grandfather and the other Iban were content to take the heads of the crew. Harry found himself looking for the little old tracker throughout the day. Where was Abik? That was often on his mind; he stopped looking for his uncle at the head of the column, but instead glanced backward and forward to see where Abik was walking. This was not easy to do. He'd see Abik one moment, but the next, when he looked, the tracker had disappeared and then reappeared minutes later in a different position in the column. Harry was unnerved and fascinated by the way the Iban tracker could master the labyrinthine depths of the forest. He wondered if ever he could prove himself to Abik and change the giggling to a smile of approval.

On the fourth day out of Pangkalan Lubang, the expedition came to a riverside settlement and government station called Fort Mary, where the District Resident kept a small peace-keeping force and dispensed justice to local tribesmen. At the outstation, aside from military barracks and the Resident's quarters, there were wharves and a row of shops, shacks really, from which Chinese merchants bartered with the jungle people. At low tide along the riverbank there were mud flats, a vast sink of decomposing weeds and dead fish in the muck, but at high tide most of the stinking debris was hidden under a flat brown surface of river water. Old cannon, their use now problematical, covered both river approaches to Fort Mary. It was gray, ugly, without a hint of Harry's romantic notion of what such an outstation in the interior might be.

That evening Harry and his uncle were invited to dine with the Resident Officer in his quarters. Actually, his quarters were a rambling shanty built on stilts with a rickety front porch where every Friday the Resident dispensed cheap medicine to the sick and chatted with visiting headmen from Dayak tribes and Malay villages.

The Resident, in white duck trousers, white cotton shirt, and gold epaulets, was a dapper little fat man with a waxed mustache, the half-moon ends of which he often twirled for emphasis when he talked. And he talked a great deal when they sat at the lamplit table with china plates and crystal glasses. That dinner table, unlike the rest of the shabby house, had a certain elegance that suggested it was something in life he truly cared about.

His servant, a sour-faced old Malay, brought course after course to the table. The Resident gave a lecture on every dish, claiming that it was entirely improper for Englishmen abroad to complain of local cuisine. "Eat what the people eat," he declared, his ruddy face beaming over a plate of stingray roasted in leaves held together by pins of coconut ribbing. Under his watchful eye, Harry ate a little of everything served. He liked the chicken fried with chilies; since coming to Borneo, he had adapted his palate to the hot spices. But he had trouble with the globefish cooked with sour fruit and tapioca, especially after the Resident pointed out that the globefish gallbladder was deadly poisonous if not properly removed. The Resident laughed heartily. "Don't worry, young man. My cook is a Melanu, and they're experts at preparing globefish." Then he took a deep swallow of wine and winked at Harry. "I'll wager you can't guess what the greatest Melanu delicacy is."

"No, sir."

"A live slug. They find it in the stumps of sago. They pinch the head off and eat it with salt."

"Alive?"

The Resident turned to Officer Windsor. "The boy has a lot to learn, hasn't he." Turning back to Harry, he said, "Alive and wriggling."

A cake made of rice flour, sugar, and grated coconut was presented for dessert. Though excessively sweet, it was the best part of the meal, and Harry had two portions, then sat back and watched the men take brandy and turn the conversation to matters other than food.

The Resident agreed with Officer Windsor that the abrupt disappearance of the Penan could signify trouble.

Harry leaned forward.

The Resident revealed that word had come in from Malay traders about Kayan restlessness in the interior. There had been quarrels between them and neighboring longhouses of Kelabit. One trader claimed that heads were being taken in skirmishes between the tribes. "If the Kayan go to war," continued the Resident, touching one end of his waxed mustache, "you can be sure they'll go looking for Iban, their natural enemy."

With a sigh he said to Harry, "I imagine for a boy your age this is adventurous and exotic. But the truth is something else." He turned to Officer Windsor. "Jolly different from what people might think, isn't it. Young man," he said to Harry, "there are terrible problems out here. The Malay is a devious fellow you can never turn your back on. The Chinese is noisy, rude, and heartless. Dayak, either Sea or Land Dayak, and especially the Iban branch of them, are all hot-tempered. It's a bloody cauldron out here, when you think of it." He poured himself another brandy. "You can't fit things here into a pattern. You have to base decisions on the momentary situation. You can't apply regulations blindly. Isn't that right, Officer Windsor?"

"Indeed it is," Uncle Julian agreed.

His ruddy face even redder after the brandy, the Resident gave Harry a brooding appraisal. "I hope, young man, you won't behave like some of the people sent out here these days. I'm sick and tired of young fellows who arrive here and expect furloughs home after only five years. In my day," he said, thumb and forefinger gripping one curled end of his mustache, "you were looked upon as insolent if you requested home leave before a decade of service. And I mean a decade spent in the outstations, on the rivers, with the natives. But then the young aren't prepared well these days. We British must be not only gentlemen but scholars as well—ornithologists, linguists, historians. It's our bounden duty if we have any pride at all in His Majesty's service. Do you know what I think of these people, the Iban and Kayan and Penan and Murut and Kelabit and Kenyah and Ukit and the rest? I think of them as naughty children whose naughtiness only makes a parent love them more. We people of high civilizations are responsible for them. Why, if it weren't for Englishmen out here, the tribals would be headed for destruction. Malay swindlers sell ceramic jars to the Iban for sums worth everything an Iban family has; most of the jars are worthless. And when the tribals come in with produce to be weighed and sold, the Chinese trick them by rigging the scales. Then, out of frustration, the tribals use poison to get even—snake venom or minute portions of powdered glass.

I've seen Malays and Chinese writhing in pain after a visit from Dayak. We Englishmen stand between them all and their utter destruction." This time he knocked back his snifter of brandy for emphasis.

After saying goodbye to the Resident, Harry and his uncle walked toward the barracks where they would spend the night.

"What did you think of the Resident?" Uncle Julian asked.

"He believes in his work."

"Indeed he does. He's a credit to English principle."

They walked a way in silence along the moon-washed river, hearing a blare of Chinese gongs and flutes from one of the shops. Finally Harry gave voice to what he was thinking. "The Resident calls them children. I mean, Abik seems more than a child. He knows a lot and speaks six languages."

Uncle Julian shrugged. "Many of them do. They must. First they learn their own language, along with at least one other native dialect. An Iban will probably know Kayan, maybe some Penan. To go into trading areas along the coast, they need two dialects of Chinese—Foochow and Hakka—and Malay. If they deal with the government, they need English, too. That's six or seven languages right there, just to get along. It's assumed."

Harry considered his uncle's words, but he still wasn't sure of his own opinion. How could you call a man a child when he spoke so many languages? Harry's withholding of agreement was enough for Uncle Julian to halt and put a hand on his shoulder.

"I hope, my boy, you understand what we must do out here. We're bringing these people civilization and in the process upholding the principles of English life and law. People like us, you and me and all the Windsors, we've had this obligation for generations. Do you understand?"

"I do," said Harry eagerly. He was convinced by his uncle's eloquence. "I won't disappoint you, Uncle."

"You needn't say that, of course. I've assumed it."

The next day Harry avoided Abik and stayed close to his uncle. After all, he was an Englishman with an Englishman's bounden duty to help these poor fellows out here. He saw Abik's skill with language and knowledge of the jungle for what they were: the necessary means for primitive people to survive. In this light, though he might learn many things from Abik, he must no longer be in awe of the tracker or care much for his opinion. For Harry now there was a larger purpose in life: to fulfill his destiny as a member of His Majesty's service.

· 5 ·

Next day the Resident was showing Harry and Officer Windsor his Reynolds & Branson camera, with isochromatic dry plates and a tripod. When the Resident explained that most natives fled when he brought out the camera, fearing he might capture their souls in the box, Harry laughed along with the two officers at this childish superstition.

A Malayan trader came to the porch, battered felt hat in hand, asking to see the Resident. A few days ago, far upriver, he was buying animal pelts from longhouses. His dugout canoe was going down a stream when suddenly he heard a whooshing sound and tiny thuds. Four blowgun darts were stuck in the dugout hull and a few more whizzed past his ear. Just then he reached a small rapids, which propelled him quickly downstream and out of range.

Had he been given any warning by the natives? asked the Resident. And who were they?

The Malay smiled sheepishly. He hadn't even seen who did the shooting. The darts simply appeared out of nowhere.

He handed over one of them. The dart was about eight

inches long, with cotton wrapped from the blunt end to about halfway down the shaft; this was to stabilize its movement through the blowgun tubing and give it a straight flight. Uncle Julian explained this to Harry. "Very accurate at short distances. The Malay was damned lucky." Then he sent the Resident's orderly for Abik, who knew about the weapons of every tribe in Borneo.

After examining the dart closely, the Iban tracker took a tiny lick of a gooey purple substance that had been smeared on the sharp tip.

"Tajam," he declared. "Poison from ipoh tree." He grimaced and spat. "Kayan use. Only Kayan." With a sneer he added, "Iban have better poison. Iban shoot better."

The Resident stroked a tip of his mustache nervously. "If this fellow was shot at by Kayan, that confirms our theory. The Penan went back in the forest because of fear."

Officer Windsor nodded in agreement. "Looks like the Kayan want heads."

He and the Resident quickly decided that tomorrow, in dugouts supplied by the station, the Windsor expedition would head upriver, taking along a few gunnysacks of salt, some iron knives, and some cheap mirrors. If possible, they'd placate the Kayan with gifts. If there were large war parties in the area, Windsor would not engage them but return to station. If there was only a small raiding party on the prowl, he might try to suppress the uprising quickly. That could mean a skirmish, taking prisoners, killing a few Kayan, and perhaps losing some of his own men.

"Where's your grin?" Uncle Julian asked his nephew in the barracks later. "I'm dashed pleased to see it's gone."

"Nothing to be grinning about, sir."

"That's right. You're getting the idea. Would you care to stay here at the outstation till we return?"

45

"No, sir, I would not."

"I had to ask out of respect for your parents." Uncle Julian sounded apologetic, as if the question had been a formality and he'd known the answer beforehand. Harry was gratified by this show of faith in his courage, though in truth he felt more than a twinge of fear.

And then that night he had a dream. He was on a ship leaving a dock. It was in England. Looking over the side at the people gathered to see the ship off, Harry saw his mother in the crowd. She was smiling and waving gaily at him, though tears rolled down her face. He waved back but was crying, too. Then he awoke, sitting bolt upright, his heart pounding. Since her death, when he dreamed of his mother, she had always crossed the same street while the same huge truck bore down on her. He hadn't seen her smiling in his dreams until now. Though afraid for him, she waved gaily and held out a locket attached to a chain. Leaning over the rail, he took it from her just as the ship sailed away.

Harry lay back on his cot, feeling calmer. He was afraid, but not so afraid that he'd stay here at the outstation. He'd go, as he should, as his mother would want him to do, to say nothing of generations of battle-hardened Windsors. More than ever, he resolved to emulate them.

The following afternoon they reached the first stop on their journey into the interior. All day Harry had looked with wonder at the river Skrang. Though less informed about the jungle than Abik, his uncle told him many things along the way. "Remember the caterpillar?" Uncle Julian said. "Well, here's another little creature who can do the same thing." He pointed to an iridescent fly poised on the dugout gunwale. "Its sting leaves a sore that might take a year to heal." Casually he brushed the insect away; it dipped toward the water and sped low over the surface. Uncle Julian was talkative, chatty, so much so that

Harry wondered if he was trying to take their minds off the danger. Uncle Julian described a black salamander used in native stews; it lived in mountain caves and made a sound like a baby crying when caught. He noticed, within the riverbank shrubbery, the thin sensitive snout of a barking deer and patiently waited until Harry saw it and a sleek head and huge limpid eyes, too; then he explained that the deer was good to eat, but Dayak would cook it only outdoors, fearful that within the confines of a longhouse its timid soul might leave its flesh and infect warriors with shyness. He pointed out flora along the riverbank, such as sundew and pitcher plants, as the twisting river led farther inland, until there were no longer the zinc roofs of isolated shacks to be seen glittering through the forest, but only mangrove swamps, driftwood, small inlets leading back into the shade of overreaching greenery. Harry felt as though he had left the planet. Often he glanced around at the dugouts to confirm that men still existed here, for suddenly he'd been plunged into a strange vast landscape that contained no trace of humanity. So he was surprised and relieved to see, around a bend in the river, a huge longhouse appear and two, perhaps three hundred people standing on the long veranda, staring down a steep embankment at the approaching boats.

It was a Kenyah longhouse.

When the expedition reached the building made of wooden planks and climbed the notched-pole ladder, Harry was gratified to see that most of the Englishmen had to shinny up its slippery length as if it were a tree. His own awkward performance probably went unnoticed. Not that he ought to care what these children of the jungle thought about his lack of skill in climbing a ladder. Reaching the veranda, he stared boldly at the smiling delegation of welcomers, both men and women, many of them with their eyebrows plucked and their earlobes stretched down in huge loops to their shoulders.

His uncle had told him that the Kenyah were the most hospitable people of Borneo, and indeed, Harry hadn't taken ten steps down the rattan floor before someone thrust a bamboo cup into his hand. "Don't drink that," warned his uncle. "It's arak and stronger than hell!"

The rest of that day passed in a waking dream for Harry. The Kenyah shoved countless native dishes at him, and when he refused the arak and rice wine, they gave him goat's milk laced with cinnamon and tamarind. Soon, he noticed, many of the Englishmen were drunk, as the jovial Kenyah hosts yelled out encouragement to drink more, more, more! There was dancing by pretty girls in sarongs and old men in beaded headgear.

A dayung appeared on the veranda with the liver of a newly slain pig in his hand. Pompously he studied the wrinkles on it, declaring after a long while that the God of War was calm and content. There would be no trouble in the area. The penghulu, headman of the longhouse, sat expressionless through the prophecy; a boy cooled his old face and stooped shoulders with a palm-leaf fan. When the soothsayer had finished, the penghulu raised his hand for silence and solemnly promised the visiting Englishmen that he would dream the necessary dream tonight and explain it to them in the morning.

This did not puzzle Harry, who had learned, first through Abik and then through his uncle, of the importance of dreams to Dayak tribes. They believed no one could become brave or rich or great unless a dream foretold it. So a dream could determine the course of an entire life. Great dreams, Abik claimed, were still spoken of by the Iban after many generations. One famous chief dreamed of visiting a spirit longhouse, another of meeting a demon hunter, another of making love to a goddess. One such dream was enough to label someone a leader of his people. Afterward, any dream of his assumed importance.

In the morning, before the expedition left the longhouse,

where many of the Englishmen had slept off the effects of arak, the penghulu described last night's dream in such rambling detail that no one could understand it, except himself. The upshot was that the dayung had correctly read the pig-liver wrinkles: Sengalang Burong, the God of War, was peacefully asleep. There was nothing to fear from any tribe, maintained the penghulu.

But after leaving the longhouse, Uncle Julian told Harry that the soothsayer and the old chief were trying to mislead them. "The Kayan and the Kenyah tend to be allies. I'm more suspicious than ever. Those shrewd old devils are covering up the truth—their friends the Kayan are out for heads."

"And it's our job to stop them."

Uncle Julian smiled. "Yes, *our* job to stop them."

For the first time, Harry truly felt that he belonged with the expedition. Not that his uncle meant for him to get into the fighting. But in a sense he was now one of them; and during the next two days, while they paddled upstream, he looked around at the men, both Englishmen and Iban, with the same feeling of solidarity that he'd felt with certain classmates in school. It was a happy time for Harry Windsor, though at moments he wondered if he'd really behave well under fire. But there was little time for him to brood about that. They left the canoes with two Englishmen, then headed again through keranga and entered yet another rain forest.

Duck Foot tried to imitate the gracefully gliding way in which Bayang moved through the forest, but she had none of his training and found herself doubly awkward because of the webbed foot that gave her a lopsided shuffling walk. In spite of her shame for slowing his progress, Duck Foot continued to feel good about this journey. She admired the young warrior, not only for his jungle skills but also for his cleverness. When they had set out in search of the white men, Bayang had startled her by heading in the opposite direction—that which the Penan hunters had taken in search of pig. It took her a while to understand what he was doing: instead of wandering aimlessly through trackless jungle in the wild hope of finding the white men, he was going to find the Penan first and learn from them exactly where to go. Bayang must have been right to do this, because shortly after turning in the direction of the Penan hunting party, he heard the call of the isit bird, which lives on spiders. Turning, he smiled at her. "A good omen."

Within two days he found the Penan. In a dense rain forest they had cleared ground and constructed a few pondoks— platforms made of saplings lashed together with vines—for temporary shelter. Though young, Bayang did not hesitate but strode into the encampment where half a dozen Penan were squatting around a campfire, roasting a pair of gibbons. Nearby, stretched out among peels of papayas and mangoes and bananas, was a python, which they had killed but not yet skinned, its slick-looking fifteen feet seeming to wriggle because of swarms of bright-winged flies that came and went in search of openings to the succulent meat within.

Duck Foot marveled at Bayang's boldness until she realized that it was not at all rash. Had he walked so abruptly into a camp of Murut or Kayan hunters, they might have killed him instantly with their spear-tipped blowguns. But the mild-mannered Penan simply looked at him appraisingly. Squatting, he took out a pouch from his knapsack of lizard skin and distributed a handful of tobacco to the Penan. Next he admired the size and beauty of the python that only they could have killed, but politely refused to share their meal, observing with the eloquence of an Iban that the gibbons, though sweet-fleshed and doubtless brought down with great skill, were hardly enough for the mouths of six such masterful hunters. Having finished with the formalities, Bayang asked questions concerning the whereabouts of the white men. The Penan answered as precisely as they could. Duck Foot understood now why they were called by other tribes the Dream People. They seemed to be in a communal trance, hardly more aware of their surroundings than a mouse deer or a lizard might be. Yet by persistence Bayang got what he came for. The Penan worked hard to remember exactly where they had seen signs of the white men. One finally recalled it was not on the Skrang but on a nearby river: some canoes; men in them heading for the Baram. Another Penan corrected him. They were not heading there, but for the place where the Balui and Kayan Rivers rise. This was as much as anyone could have learned from such spellbound people. Bayang was truly the son of an Iban headman, she told herself. And who was traveling with him on this most important journey of his life? She, merely Tambong, whom they called Duck Foot, was traveling with him.

And now perhaps they'd be rewarded for the long arduous trek, because today near the headwaters of those two rivers they had found campfires and other evidence of white men. There would be no difficulty following the party now. Those white ghosts cleared a path through the jungle as brazenly wide as that made by a passing troop of orangutans. Duck Foot caressed the hook stone—a curved black pebble—that she wore around one wrist for luck. For the first time in days she had noticed the muscles in Bayang's back relax as he led the way slowly, methodically through the jungle. Lately he had been worried by his inability to dream. Though he never complained to her, Duck Foot was certain of his disappointment. She had stopped asking him if he dreamed, because every time she did so, his only reply was a deep scowl. Now that they were on the trail of the white men, perhaps such good fortune was as good as a dream. She stroked the hook stone tenderly and limped onward.

· 6 ·

H arry was getting into the habit, when they halted for the
day, of going off by himself as if to test his ability to be
alone in the jungle. Not that he went far. It was said among the
men that no one went alone out there, no one, not even the
most experienced tracker. If a Dayak set out alone on a journey, people who met him on the way would think that he was
crazy—or worse, that he was bali saleng, the evil black spirit in
human disguise, for only spirits went alone in the jungle.

Once Harry had got momentarily lost, not more than a few
hundred yards from camp. For a nerve-racking minute he
hadn't been sure which way to go; the jungle had a way of
repeating itself so that he couldn't remember if this was a new
tree or one he'd just recently passed. Dread surged through
him, as his uncle's words came to mind: "People sometimes
think they know their way in the jungle, and when they dis-
cover they don't it's too late. They're lost forever. It happens all
the time to Malays and Chinese. Not to Dayak perhaps, unless
you get them away from their neighborhoods. Jungle is treach-
erous, my boy. Respect its power. Believe in its trickery."

Fortunately, Harry had faced the panic of being lost only once. In searching around, he had managed to locate a few of his own boot prints in the muddy earth; they set him in the right direction and led him back to camp. But the next time he might not be so lucky. Testing himself away from the group was one thing; going too far out was another. So now he went only as far as he could go and still hear faint sounds of camp life in the distance.

Today, however, he wanted to find water. The march had been especially long and hot and for at least half of it he'd wished for a cool dip in one of the ponds that so contrast in Borneo with the ovenlike rain forest surrounding them. In his search for water, Harry had gone farther than usual, ignoring caution in his need to cool off. His reward for being somewhat bold was that suddenly he came to a long, narrow pond canopied by mossy limbs and a network of huge leaves. From overhead came the racketing *tuk tuk* sound of brown barbets, odd-looking birds with big thick bodies, large heads, and short legs. Harry had learned their call along with those of a dozen other common birds. As he approached, Harry saw a blue-throated bee-eater snapping up insects as it flew in graceful curves above the brown surface of the pond.

Before he reached its bank, Harry was throwing off his sweaty clothes, strewing them on the moss-covered ground and along knobby root systems. From his neck Harry removed a chain. Attached to it was a locket with an oval painting of his mother inside. In a round frame, protected by a hinged case of beaten gold, the portrait was Harry's most valued record of his mother. She had given it to him two years earlier for his birthday. Kissing him as she hung it around his neck, she had exclaimed, "So there! Remember how I was before turning old and gray." Often, since her death, Harry had looked at this picture and spoken to it. "So there! You'll never turn old and gray." It had given him an odd measure of solace, a kind of defiant pride in thinking that while fate had done a terrible thing, it had also prevented his mother from losing her youthful beauty.

Placing the locket on top of his shirt, Harry went down to the water and waded in. The coolness thrilled him. Glancing up at the overreaching leaves, Harry let out a crisp little whoop of delight, then ducked beneath the water and came up swimming.

Startled, Duck Foot wondered if the white boy she was watching had just been possessed by a water demon. She'd never heard an Iban make such a noise. But then she'd never seen such white skin before. Duck Foot had never imagined that a white man would be so *white*. Bayang seemed to pay no attention to the strange boy in the pond. Instead he crept closer to the clothes and shoes and other objects on the ground only a few steps away from where they'd been hiding. They had tracked the white party all afternoon, and when the youngest of them left the others and walked through the forest, they had followed him.

Now Bayang crept forward, belly pressed against the mossy earth, to wiggle his way toward the things dropped by the white boy, who was splashing gaily in the water. Duck Foot watched nervously while her companion picked up each item, studied it, and put it down. He worked methodically as if contemptuous of being seen. She expected this, for an Iban warrior should never show haste or fear in the presence of others. At last Bayang wiggled back to her, something gripped in his hand. Fumbling with it until it fell open into halves like a shell, Bayang gasped, as did Duck Foot, at what they found inside. It was a woman's face, a white woman's face, smiling at them from a circle; her hair was dark red, like the color of a fire ant. When Bayang pressed the halves together, there was a snapping sound and he had to fumble again to open it. "Obat," he whispered, and Duck Foot agreed that surely this was something of potent magic.

Glancing toward the pond, where the mad white boy was still flailing his arms and legs, she saw something beyond him. She gave a stifled cry and gripped Bayang's arm, so that he, too, saw it: a long gray log move a few inches from the bank into the water.

Standing up from behind the tree where they were hiding, Bayang raised his blowgun and waved it back and forth, high over his head. When the white boy failed to see this, Bayang added a long deep call, like that of a water buffalo. The startled white boy stopped flailing and stood up in chest-deep water. Though looking straight at the twosome, he didn't see them until Bayang deliberately stepped out in the clearing, waved his blowgun again, and yelled, this time in the high-pitched nasal way of a honey bear. Then he jabbed the spear tip of his blowgun several times, hard, in the direction of the log, which had moved again, with its long length halfway into the pond.

When the white boy stood there in the water, mouth open, gawking, Duck Foot told herself that surely he was mad; a spirit must have entered him and possessed his soul.

Taking a few steps toward the pond, Bayang pointed his blowgun directly at the log, whose long gray shape had slid nearly all the way into the water.

Then the white boy seemed to understand. Glancing over his shoulder, he saw the raised nostrils and eyes of the crocodile as it began gliding toward him. With a shriek of fear, the boy thrashed his way to the shore, moving with an alacrity that belied Duck Foot's estimate of him as crazy. He reached the shore and scrambled from the pond in good time to deter the crocodile, who blinked twice before sinking below the surface.

The white boy slipped on the mossy wet ground and fell to one knee.

At that moment Bayang's intent gaze met the white boy's blue-eyed look of astonishment. Having never seen blue eyes before, Bayang took a step backward without thinking. Duck Foot saw this and wondered if somehow the white boy had tricked an Iban warrior into a small act of cowardice.

All three were awestruck. Then, regaining his composure, Bayang wheeled and trotted away, with the stolen obat of magic in his hand and with Duck Foot limping along behind him.

When Harry sheepishly reported that natives had surprised him while he'd been swimming in a pond, Uncle Julian observed sourly that he'd been lucky they hadn't been Kayan warriors, or he might have taken a poisoned dart in the back. But it was his uncle's turn to be surprised when Harry explained how the native—about his own age and accompanied by a girl—had warned him of a crocodile.

"Your age? There's not a native settlement hereabouts for miles. What in hell are a Dayak boy and a girl doing out here alone? Well, at least they were friendly enough to warn you. Some are, you know. I suspect they saved your life."

Harry nodded, but then added, his lips trembling, "They took the locket my mother gave me."

Uncle Julian put a comforting hand on his shoulder. "I'm sorry, lad. I know how you treasured it."

Harry said nothing more. He didn't want pity, and yet nothing he possessed had meant more to him than that locket.

Next day on the trail, all Harry could think of was the loss of that locket. The two natives had taken nothing else. He had a good knife on his belt, solid hiking boots, a little pair of binoculars. Why hadn't they taken such things, all of which might be used in the jungle, instead of something worthless to them like an Englishwoman's portrait in a locket?

He caught himself that day glancing sideways at Abik as the tracker moved up and down the column of marchers. He studied the little man, who wore a deadly parang tied about his waist with a thong of rhino hide. These Dayak, whatever their tribe, were more than naughty children, as the Resident described them. They were thieves without honor. By the end of that day's march, Harry had quite forgotten how the native boy had stood up and waved a blowgun and called out to warn him. He had forgotten the crocodile, too. All he remembered was searching frantically through rotten leaves. And he no longer liked Abik.

Miles away, while Duck Foot smoked a squirrel for dinner in a section of bamboo, Bayang turned the obat around in his callused fingers. Every now and then, awkwardly, he'd flip the clasp and open the two halves of the shell and thoughtfully regard the woman with the white face and red hair. So the spirits had done more than give him a sign; they had provided him with the sort of magic that could help him reenter the dream world and find the Big Fish. This might be the face of the Goddess of Sleep. Old dayungs used to say she ruled the Land of Dreams, and at her pleasure gave a man good dreams and at her displeasure sent him nightmares. No one had ever seen her face, though the soothsayers maintained that she had human features but skin like clouds and hair the color of dark blood. She belonged to no one among the gods but protected her independence jealously. It did no good to pray to her, unless she herself had decided you were worth her goodwill. Neither good nor evil, she could not be placated or tempted by gifts of food and ceramic jars. All you could do, so the dayungs claimed, was hope for her mercy. If you had that, you had the most powerful of spirits protecting you. She was even more powerful than the God of War, who lived in the sky in the form of Lang Sengalang Burong, the Brahminy kite, the omen bird that liked to swoop down and punish men for wrongdoing.

With the obat of the Goddess of Sleep in his possession, Bayang believed that he could never fail, after entering the Dream World, to find the Big Fish and reach his destiny. Looking over at Duck Foot, he announced with pride that the journey was almost finished. He had what they had come for. He told her what he'd been thinking.

Her answering silence disturbed him. Usually the girl nodded in agreement with what he said, but now she merely stared at the hind legs of the cooking squirrel, visible at one end of the bamboo tube.

Finally, impatiently, he asked for her opinion.

Turning to him, but glancing at the ground instead of his face while she spoke, Duck Foot gave him the opinion he asked for but would not like. She was not sure if the obat was good or evil or if the red-haired white woman's face was that of a goddess or a demon. Everyone knew that the bali saleng took many human disguises. Often he wore blue clothing or hid his pointed teeth with which he sucked blood from human necks. But sometimes he appeared as a beautiful woman who tempted unwary men. Could this red-haired woman be evil?

"He knows. The white boy knows," replied Bayang with a scowl. "But if this obat is evil, why did he have its likeness with him?"

"Who knows?" Duck Foot lifted both hands in a gesture of helplessness. "But can you trust any dream that comes from this thing"—she pointed to the locket, its chain dangling from his fingers—"till you know it's good? What of tricks? What if you dreamed of a soul's journey to the Land of the Dead? I know of such things. I learned when I crawled under the dayung's house and listened through the floor to what he said about the soul's journey. It's made when you die. Or if you dream of making it and believe in the dream, you die. Dead and dreaming of death become the same. The dead and the dreamers wander a long time until they come to the top of a mountain, where they look down on places where each of the dead go. Like Apo Laggan, where people who die of sickness live as they did in life. Or the Lake of Blood, where warriors go. Or the Swamp of Dreamers, where people tricked into dreaming of death go if they let the dream kill them. There's no sunlight in the swamp, only trees forever and beneath them mud too thick to walk through and mosquitoes that never rest. From the mountaintop the seven selves of the dead look down—the knife soul, the tobacco-box soul, the blowgun soul, the dart-case soul, the rice soul, the temporary soul, the lasting soul—all of them howling at what they see below. Then they come down to cross the River of the Dead—"

Impatiently Bayang interrupted her. "What has this to do with the Goddess of Sleep?"

"It might not be the goddess. It could be a demon who'll trick you into climbing the mountain and believing in the dream until it kills you. You could be tricked into thinking you'll find the Big Fish there instead of death." There were tears in her eyes. "I don't want you to die. That thing"—she was staring at the locket—"is not yet known for good or bad."

"Well, then, how can we know?" he asked gravely.

There was a long silence. Then the girl met his eyes. "We find the white men again."

Bayang, surprised, merely repeated her words. "We find the white men again."

"And the boy who had this thing. He'll know its meaning."

"Yes, I see. If it's good, I can trust it. If it's bad, I give it back to him."

"No," said Duck Foot. "Destroy it. Or he might use it against you."

Bayang nodded in agreement. "So we'll find the white men again."

"And what of that boy?"

Bayang stared at the obat. "We take him and keep him with us till we know this for good or bad." When she was silent again, Bayang told her gruffly to say what she wanted to say.

"What if he tricks us? Can white men be trusted?"

Bayang glanced around at the wall of forest, then up at the high branches of a camphor tree. "We'll have omens to guide us. We'll have signs. Birds will tell us. Falling trees will tell us."

"What if you dream while on the way?"

Bayang considered that. He shook his head glumly. "I will not believe in the soul's journey."

"But what if it's another dream? Will you listen to it?"

"I don't know."

"Under the dayung's house, I'd hear them through the boards," said Duck Foot. "Once I heard one of them warn the others never to believe in certain dreams. Never in a dream if it came in the colors of the jungle or a dream if it came from something like a new charm stone you hadn't worn yet or a dream that spoke to you in a voice you didn't know or a dream that came from anything found on a long journey like ours—a Bejelai. The dayung warned them to wait for other signs before trusting such dreams."

"I understand. I won't believe in any dreams that come from this." He hefted the obat, snapped it shut, and put its chain around his neck. "Not till we know if it's to be trusted." Bayang sighed. "It's not easy to find the Big Fish. But then, all great dreams lead first to mystery before they tell you what is real."

· 7 ·

H arry didn't understand Officer Windsor. What had come over his uncle, Harry wondered, as the tall, florid officer glared or shouted at him, barking out orders to do this or that. It was as if Harry were being punished for something. He was given a rifle and put on early morning guard duty. When something had to be cleared or lifted, Officer Windsor signaled him with great impatience to lend a hand. He had to wash pots, help the cook. He was always on the late afternoon detail that cleared away brush for setting up camp. It seemed that his duties multiplied each day, and nothing he did could satisfy Officer Windsor or bring even a faint smile to that severe taskmaster's face.

Harry worked so hard and felt so exhausted that he rarely thought of the locket anymore. He had worn it around his neck in another world in another age. He was no more than a slave now who did the bidding of a strange man who used to be his uncle. After a week of increasingly hard work, he could scarcely remember the pattern of gold tracery around the frame of his mother's portrait in the locket. The truth was that Harry felt harder and leaner than ever before; each day of adversity burnished his skills until he was doing more than his share among the men. Though he hadn't much time to notice it, his fellow Englishmen were giving him grudging smiles of approval. And had they been asked, they might have said, "Well, the lad may be the officer's nephew, but he's a splendid chap that pulls his own weight."

Even the Iban trackers gave him a measure of respect by ignoring his awkwardness when he slipped on a root system and fell. That did not include Abik, however, who continued to giggle with contemptuous amusement at Harry's clumsiness. Once Harry toppled over a rotting log into a little pond, facedown. When he came up spluttering, he saw Abik grinning. But when their eyes met, the Iban said, "Are you angry that I laugh?"

"You have no right to laugh."

"Right?" The word seemed to puzzle Abik.

"You aren't in charge," Harry said coldly.

The Iban stared a moment longer, then turned and walked haughtily away as if Harry no longer existed. His disdain used to be modified by a concern for the white boy's welfare. This abrupt change in the Iban's behavior puzzled Harry until it struck him that the tracker was hurt. What had happened? Harry had been treating the Iban coldly after the lesson in colonial responsibility from the Resident and Uncle Julian. The "ignorant child of the jungle" had instantly perceived the change in Harry's attitude and had changed his own accordingly. Abik matched aloofness with aloofness, pride with pride, superiority with superiority.

One evening after supper many of the men lit up pipes and cheroots, filling the perfumed air of the jungle with acrid tobacco smoke. Sitting by himself, Harry was surprised when Abik came along and squatted beside him, rump nearly touching the ground in Iban fashion. Abik nudged the boy's arm and with a fierce grin asked him if he knew what was happening. When Harry merely stared at him, Abik laughed as if he'd just been told a joke. You don't know anything, Abik told the boy. About what? Harry asked. As usual, they spoke in a mixture of English, Iban, and gesture.

Abik looked up at the dusky sky, a few strands of cloud giving the illusion of threading themselves through the trees. "Watch what is," the Iban tracker said in a slow measured way, then he got up and went off.

Watch what is. Harry thought about that; in fact, it was the last thing he thought about before falling asleep. What surrounded him was the thrumming constancy of insect sound and the blunt crashing of monkeys above and wild pigs below and the broom-beating-a-rug sound of flying foxes settling themselves on fruit tree branches, and the call of the black hornbill (Harry could now distinguish it from the call of other hornbills): the *te gok te gok te gok,* beginning low and becoming shriller until it ended in a laughing cackle. He heard what was there in the absolute darkness.

The next day, however, he watched what was, and what was seemed to be nothing more or less than Abik, who came and went like an apparition, vanishing in jungle and reappearing on the trail with the suddenness of a puff of smoke, his bronzed skin glistening from sweat, his wrinkled face puckered into a studious frown as he spoke in whispers with Officer Windsor, a few Englishmen, and the other trackers. What was happening had to do with Abik. Watching him was watching what was.

Harry's attitude toward the Iban, since the expedition began, had swung from one extreme to the other, from blind admiration to cool disdain. Forced now to acknowledge Abik's mysterious importance to the expedition, Harry could no longer maintain his aloofness. During a halt, feeling a bit sheepish but also determined, he went over to Abik, who was squatting in the shade, smoking a large black cheroot.

"Please tell me," Harry said in English, "what is happening? You alone know. I see that from watching you."

Abik stared at him through narrowed eyes a few moments before replying. Then he smiled, as if the past two weeks had never happened and he still had the white boy under his protective wing. He explained what was happening by asking questions, in Iban or English or with gestures. Had Tuan Harry lifted his eyes lately and looked at the jungle? At the dart stuck in a tree? No? Hadn't he seen the dart? Had he seen the pipe ash yesterday on the bank of the stream? The toe print in the mud? The few shreds of loincloth hanging on a thornbush? Hadn't he seen some of the many signs of another party in the neighborhood?

To cover his embarrassment at having seen nothing, instead of replying to these questions Harry asked one. "Who are these people?"

"Kayan."

"Have you seen them?"

"No. Only the signs."

"Is it a war party?"

Abik nodded.

"A war party," Harry repeated. "Are there many in it?"

Abik held up both hands, opening and shutting them three times: about thirty. Then he explained that the dart stuck in a tree had been painted red, which for the Kayan was the color of war. The Kayan used such a dart only against their enemies.

"Are we their enemies?"

"Iban always their enemy," Abik said proudly, jabbing his chest with a bony finger. "You only for small time."

"So their enemy right now is our expedition?"

Abik grinned happily.

"Will they attack us?"

Abik shrugged as if such a question had little meaning. He made it clear to Harry that Kayan actions depended on the need for heads. If they had taken a few, they might go home. If they had taken none, most likely they'd remain in the jungle, circling around, until they did. He estimated that the Kayan were a day's march ahead, and unless they sent a scout back to see if they were being followed, they might very well continue to the far reaches of the Balui River, where they'd take out their anger and frustration on wandering bands of Penan or Murut. Abik stared thoughtfully into the dense maze of rain forest before continuing. Then he placed one hand on the scabbard of his parang. Knowing the Kayan as he did, declared Abik, he was almost sure they'd send a scout back.

"Meaning they'll find us?"

Abik nodded with a bright smile.

That happy smile unnerved Harry, who realized that the Iban tracker was spoiling for a fight. Englishmen of honor never ran from one, but they didn't spoil for it either. Only fools did that. And yet, was Abik, this skilled man of the jungle, really a fool?

"How will we know if they find us?" Harry asked finally.

Abik whipped his parang from its scabbard. "Kayan very good. Shoot first, then we know they find us."

"You mean, we can expect an ambush?"

The concept of an ambush took a little time for Abik to understand. Then he waved the parang and repeated the English word enthusiastically. "Ah, ambuuuush!" He thrust into the humid air fiercely with his long knife.

Harry was appalled by the Iban's boastful and devil-may-care attitude about an engagement. It had the effect of draining away some of Harry's own self-confidence. He fought hard to maintain it. Between his uncle and the Iban tracker, Harry felt trapped in thankless labor and the prospect of behaving like a coward. Of course, if he must, he could do the work, however unpleasant; it was cowardice that he feared. Perhaps it was better that his father was not alive to hear about it in case it happened, in case it . . . went badly if they encountered the Kayan. It was difficult enough to have his uncle witnessing his behavior. Harry winced at the thought of that cold-eyed man standing behind him during an ambush. He imagined Uncle Julian declaring, "I should have left you at the outstation. Better that than seeing you run at the first sign of trouble!"

Harry had a poor night's sleep and awoke bleary-eyed, grumpy, and scared. His imaginary scene with Uncle Julian carried the force of reality. He felt obliged to defend his personal honor. One of these days he'd stop obeying his uncle blindly and stand up for himself. He wouldn't be treated like a slave anymore. He'd have it out with Uncle Julian even if it meant being insubordinate.

A confrontation with his uncle took place sooner than Harry had expected, but it was much different from what he had imagined.

The expedition was on the trail in single file after a brief but fierce rain shower had soaked them through. Rampant swarms of insects appeared as usual after the downpour, and Harry felt a wing brushing against his open left eye, a tiny body lighting in his right nostril and flying out again, while his entire face was a landing field for translucent, buzzing little things that seemed to be seeking entrance into the dark center of his mind. At this unpleasant moment one of the Englishmen came up and jerked his thumb toward the head of the column. "Officer Windsor wants you, lad."

Harry lumbered forward through the mud until reaching his uncle, who had just brought the march to a halt. Seeing his nephew, Officer Windsor waved him off the narrow path and into a stand of bamboo for a private talk.

"My pistol takes a beating in this climate," Uncle Julian said, removing his .45 from its holster. "It needs cleaning every day. From now on, after the evening meal, I want you to clean it thoroughly."

Harry barked, "Sir!" He had learned this way of acknowledging an order from the other Englishmen.

"I noticed you do a poor job of cleaning your rifle. When you're not sure of doing something right, ask for help."

"Sir!"

"Tonight I'll show you the right way to clean guns."

"Sir!" He felt his uncle's eyes appraising him.

"Is there something you wish to say, Harry?"

Harry could hold it back no longer. "I don't know what I've done, Uncle Julian. You haven't told me what's wrong. What you do is give me more work, which is all right in itself, I can do it, I'm not afraid to work, sir, but I wish I knew why I'm singled out, I—"

Uncle Julian gripped his arm. "Wait, lad. I'll say this only once, so listen. Everyone loses something dear. It can't be helped. So what's important is going on from the loss, and the only way I know to do that is to work." He dropped his hand from Harry's arm. "Enough of this talk. Get back in line. We have another hour of march ahead of us before making camp."

By the time Harry returned to his place in the column, everyone was on the move, sloshing through the muddy rain forest. Harry could see leeches dropping from wet leaves. They lighted on exposed necks and arms; hands flicked at them to brush the wrigglers off before they dug in. Mechanically, like the rest of the men, Harry swept his own hand across his arm. He no longer even grimaced at the slippery, churning bodies of the leeches. They were part of the jungle. He could no more change that than stop the sun from rising. Flicking and stumbling, he kept his place in line and marched awhile before fully grasping what his uncle had meant by their talk. All the added work and responsibility had resulted from his loss of the locket. It was Uncle Julian's way of helping him. Father would have done the same, Harry thought. It was the Windsor way of handling trouble and loss—don't brood about it, just get on with the job.

Harry was still thinking about his uncle—with a return of affection and trust—when a shout from the trail up ahead had everyone lurching to a halt.

Gunfire.

Harry was near the middle of the column, so he could see nothing at either end of it. When there was more gunfire, this time from behind him, he understood in an instant that they had been ambushed. Where was Abik? He hadn't seen Abik in a long time. He needed Abik to tell him what was happening!

Harry then heard a strange whooshing noise, and a distinct little thud, and saw a sliver of wood appear suddenly on the shirt of an Iban named Rentap just in front of him. The slender piece of wood, its end wrapped in cotton, quivered at the center of a widely spreading circle of blood. The bright red look of it was so vivid that Harry felt he was seeing everything in slow motion, with infinite time to contemplate each portion of the expanding horror. Rentap's hand came around his back, vainly seeking to grip the dart and pull it out, but then he sank down on his knees, as if the wind had been knocked out of him, and toppled into the mud.

People were scrambling off the path, escaping into dense thickets, and without a moment's thought Harry went with them. He followed just behind an Englishman who thrashed blindly into undergrowth, slashing his arms on thornbushes. Harry slashed his own, too, but didn't feel it. His entire being was focused upon what he heard: cries of pain filled the thick air and a whooping sound not unlike that of gibbons but different, too—a human sound—and the metallic pop of guns going off.

He was running. Where had the man gone whom he was following? In such a tangle of tree and bush you could lose sight of someone in an instant. Harry had. He was alone! He felt utterly isolated from everything but an implacable fear that kept his arms moving, his legs pumping, his mouth gasping for air. Stumbling forward and parting some huge fronds, he stared directly ahead at a rippling stream where a large monitor lizard, nearly six feet long, kerplunked into the water like a fallen tree trunk. Catching his breath, trying to compose himself, Harry was staring at the gray wrinkled back of the huge lizard when something told him he was being watched.

Harry thought of running, but to his utter dismay he felt as though he couldn't move. He even looked down to see if he was standing in quicksand. He just couldn't get his legs to obey the command to move one in front of the other. All he could do was feel, and what he felt was a kind of icy sensation spreading sluggishly but rapidly through his body: legs, chest, jaws, head.

Something was there, ready to kill him. If he couldn't move now, he'd be dead in a few more seconds. Abruptly it occurred to Harry that he still had his gun. He could defend himself. But before he could unsling the rifle and raise it, the faint sound of a twig cracking made him turn and look through the foliage into the face of someone about his own age, into a face he had seen before.

There was the same blowgun, its spear tip pointed at his throat. He backed away and the blowgun came forward, until the boy holding it appeared, both hands clutching the long weapon near the mouth.

When the boy nodded vigorously, Harry dropped his own

hand from the rifle butt. Another tense nod demanded that Harry slip the sling from his shoulder until the rifle fell to the ground. The spear point moved, indicating direction. Harry turned where it wanted him to go, and at a stumbling trot, urged on by the point nicking his shoulderblade, careened forward through the jungle until he could no longer hear any cries or gunfire, but only the rapid, heavy sound of his own breathing.

· 8 ·

D uck Foot was following the progress of sunlight as it
reached from one branch to the next to the next in a tall
camphor tree, inching its way along like a slow-footed sloth
with an entire day to get from one side of a tree to the other.
Back home, she might be steaming chips of wood from such
a tree and collecting the oil that oozed out. There would be
other girls there, too, and though they might have little to say
to her, at least they'd be there, chirping like birds, allowing her
to feel comfortable in their presence even if they didn't feel
comfortable in hers. Now she sat alone and waited without
anything to do. Bayang had positioned her near a small river,
hidden in the foliage of a hillside. When he left, the sunlight
had filtered straight down upon a termite nest, a knobby mass
of clay almost as tall as she was. Sunlight now slanted beyond
the camphor tree and against the pink petals of an orchid
growing from the heart of a rattan palm. The sun had swung
itself from overhead through myriad shadowy branches, cross-
ing at last to the little clearing where she huddled at the base
of a wild rubber tree. Her webbed foot, bare, shone darkly like
cinnamon in the sun's rays.

Bayang had been gone a long time. But before leaving, he had warned her to expect such a wait.

That had been this morning, after he ritually cut his finger with the anak parang and squeezed blood out while evoking aid from Lang Sengalang Burong. Bayang had awakened in a hopeful mood because last night he'd dreamed of holding on to a rock over a gorge. Holding on in a dream made it a good dream. Before he left this morning, they had discussed it at length, deciding finally that Bayang could trust what the dream told him. It hadn't been sent by the Goddess of Sleep, because her redheaded presence never appeared, either to give advice or to enchant him. This was Duck Foot's belief, and he came to share it.

A good dream could mean success today. A good dream could put the white boy in the middle of the column. "Yes," Bayang had affirmed with a determined smile, "the dream must put him in the middle."

"And you asked Lang Sengalang Burong for help. The dream and the god together are powerful. He should be in the middle."

"Yes," agreed Bayang, gripping the shaft of the long blowgun. "This is good."

Yesterday had not been good. He and Duck Foot had followed in the direction marked by the Penan message, which brought them to the great Balui River. The white men would surely come to it, because it was their habit to keep within sight of great rivers. They could not take too much jungle. Following the Balui, hoping to find the white men, Bayang had discovered instead a band of Kayan warriors yesterday. The Kayan were wandering through a neighborhood in which he expected to find the white men. Heavily painted and wearing hornbill feathers in their hair and monkey skins across their chests, they were clearly on the lookout for heads—any heads.

It happened to some of the Dayak tribes. His father, with contempt, had explained it to him. There were restlessness and discontent in a longhouse and certain people felt they were better than others, and to solve their problems—or rather, to forget them for a while—they got a war party together and went searching for the comforting bond that came from taking heads. This was not the Iban way, Father had maintained. The Iban did not keep slaves, nor was any man superior to his neighbor, so there were no such squabbles in an Iban long-house. If the Iban fought, it was for other reasons.

As for the Kayan war party, tomorrow they'd easily find a band of whites whose clumsiness in the jungle rivaled that of two-horned rhinoceroses. Locating those loud Englishmen who left debris and wide muddy paths behind them, to say nothing of footprints and campfires, would take little skill. Even the Kayan, better on water than on land, could find them. It was as certain as the sun coming up.

Although the dreaded Kayan were nearby, Duck Foot was not afraid. They might find white men, but not a tracker like Bayang. From Bayang's way of moving through the jungle, she knew how well he'd learned from his father and other Iban warriors. He possessed the skills of a true jungle man, so that she need only follow—trust and follow.

After they watched the Kayan halt for the day and begin making camp, to Duck Foot's surprise Bayang went still farther into the jungle. He felt strongly that the white men were close by. According to the Penan message, they were heading in this direction and most likely would follow the line of a river in the neighborhood until it reached the Balui. He was unfamiliar with the area, so he did not know the location of its many rivers, yet, sighting a flock of kingfishers in the sky, he saw them as a providential omen and headed in the direction of their flight. His faith in the omen was well founded. It was nearly dusk when they came upon the white men setting up camp at the edge of a small river. That river, if followed, would come within calling distance of the Kayan in less time than it took a deer to die of poisoned darts.

Lying in tall grass at the edge of the clearing, Duck Foot searched among the white men until she located the white boy. He was working at removing brush so that tents could be pitched. When Duck Foot had last seen the white boy, he'd been naked and his body had seemed pale, wispy. He surely looked bigger now, older, and his sweaty back was much broader than that of Bayang. There was a tinge of red in his hair that reminded her of the Goddess of Sleep. Was he an antu buyo spirit in disguise? It could be so.

Would Bayang try to take him after sunset? Weren't there too many armed men in the camp? Asking such a question would be cowardly and cause him to lose respect for her. She must say nothing, no matter what he decided. So with relief she saw Bayang motioning for her to follow him away from there.

"Tomorrow it happens," he told her when they'd crept beyond earshot of the camp. They made their own camp about half the distance between the two groups. Tomorrow both groups would follow the banks of rivers, Bayang explained, that would finally meet at the Balui. But they'd never reach the Balui, because by then the Kayan, sending out scouts, would know the whereabouts of the white men. They'd study the ground and prepare their attack to begin somewhere along the trail, which would give them an advantage. Where the narrow path curved or moved uphill was always a good place. Or they'd strike immediately after a rain shower, when there were mud and mist and annoying heat. When the Kayan did attack, Bayang declared, he'd use the opportunity to take the white boy.

While they chewed on smoked monkey meat, Bayang told

her his plan, offering as much detail as if she'd been a fellow warrior.

Duck Foot was so proud of being worthy of his trust she nearly lost track of what he said.

First he explained the Kayan method of attack. They hit both ends of a column, ignoring the middle. This allowed them to put their entire force at only two places. The object was to kill someone quickly. If they could drag two or three bodies away after a brief fight, they'd have the heads they wanted. Then, if they wished to go back for more, the people who had escaped from the middle of the column would have reassembled and gone on, providing other heads for the taking. It was like harvesting bananas—you took what you needed and came back later if not satisfied.

This was not the Iban way, he declared proudly. Though the Iban wanted heads, they wanted victory more. The Iban did not, like the Kayan, believe that taking heads was everything. Being a brave man in battle was everything. For the Kayan, it was better to take a head and be a coward than to be brave and not take one. So they fought for possessions, not for a warrior's pride. What he told Duck Foot was nothing new to her; it was a traditional Iban view. Yet rarely did a warrior speak of such matters to women, and so she listened intently, like someone unacquainted with the fiercely proud spirit of the Iban.

Tomorrow, Bayang continued, the Kayan would do as they always did: attack in front and behind. If the white boy walked in the middle of the column, he'd have a good chance to get away, though a stray dart might hit him. Bayang opened both hands out in a gesture of finality. "I'll be close by and take him if he gets away."

"What if he's in front or behind?"

"They'll be finishing the attack before he barely knows it's taking place." Bayang shook his head grimly. "The Kayan will

surely kill him. So a god must put him in the middle where he'll
be safer. I'll ask help from Lang Sengalang Burong."

Duck Foot hoped for him a good dream that night. And her
hope had come true with his dream of holding on to a rock
over a deep gorge. But now the wait for his return had become
almost unbearable. Sunlight was sinking below the trees, leaving within the dim bowls of foliage the dark liquid of night
shadows. If he didn't come soon, it would be totally dark and
even a tracker like Bayang would have difficulty moving
through jungle that he didn't know well, without familiar
things to guide him. Would he become lost? That possibility
terrified Duck Foot. She thought of him wandering farther and
farther away through a moonless night, led by demons toward
the Land of the Dead. Antu buyo, evil spirits in the darkness,
lying in wait. Antu buyo, who blinded men and suffocated
them with fear. Antu buyo . . . antu buyo . . .

Duck Foot had started to doze when abruptly a sound
brought her fully to consciousness—and there stood Bayang,
smiling, and beside him, nearly a head taller, the scowling
white boy, hands tied behind his back with a rattan thong.

Sitting propped against a tree, hands pressed against the rough
bark, Harry watched his captor eat termites that the girl must
have cooked during the day. The warrior stuffed them in like
nuts. Harry became aware of his own hunger, which grew
ravenous. When the warrior, turning suddenly, stretched out a
dark hand that offered a half-dozen grubs, without hesitation
Harry opened his mouth and let the grimy hand push the
termites in. They tasted faintly like smoked fish. He licked his
lips and opened his mouth for more when the warrior offered
another handful. When the warrior leaned toward him, Harry
smelled the loamy odor of humid jungle.

Having fed him something, the warrior seemed to forget

Harry and turned to whisper to the girl, who warily kept her distance from the captive.

Hunger appeased, Harry thought of something else. What he thought about was his own cowardice. Instead of holding his ground, he'd run blindly. It gave him no solace to realize that many of the others ran, too: cowardice was cowardice. Was his uncle still alive? How many of the expedition had been killed? Had they been wiped out? Was he the only survivor? These questions vied for attention in his mind with a certainty that the Kayan meant to murder him. The young warrior and the girl were holding him until the war party returned. Then in some ghastly ritual the Kayan would most likely behead him.

Fear moved thickly through his veins like an ice floe, the big, sluggish sheets of ice that his father used to describe from an Arctic expedition he'd made when scarcely older than Harry was now. Harry knew at last what fear felt like—real fear, the fear that consumed every moment. It wasn't knifelike. It didn't make him want to scream. He understood now that real fear was cold, numbing, as heavy and irresistible as an avalanche of snow. Yet he somehow managed to push it aside just enough for his mind to fill up with something else—with the resolve to be brave. If the war party decided to kill him, he'd have a second chance to show the courage of an Englishman, of a Windsor. But he wished to die wearing the locket that hung now around the neck of his captor. That was his second resolve: to ask for it before they decapitated him.

Fear and determination vied in Harry's mind long after the sun had set and left the small clearing in darkness. He was lulled by the steady whispering of his captor and the Kayan girl who sat opposite him. There was no moon, no light whatsoever. Without anything to see, Harry gave himself over to listening. There was the thrum of human voices, interrupted by birdcalls and animal cries, but mostly there was a chorus of insects so impenetrable that it assumed the bland consistency of utter silence, and so in such a bower of silence abruptly he fell asleep.

Sunlight opened his eyes. He had slept soundly in spite of his rattan bonds. Hampered by them, Harry struggled awkwardly into a sitting position. He stared ahead, at first uncomprehendingly, then acutely aware of the locket on the young warrior's chest. The girl was squatting over a tiny fire, a thin spiral of smoke going up the trunk of the camphor tree like the sinuous body of a snake. With her back toward Harry, she was talking to the warrior loud enough for Harry to overhear. To his surprise he understood some of what she was saying. The girl was speaking Iban. But then he recalled the fluency with language of all these Dayak people. They spoke one another's languages as well as Chinese, Malay, and possibly English. So far, realized Harry, he'd not tried to communicate with his captor, who hadn't tried with him either.

Harry decided to maintain his silence, at least for a while, at least until the war party turned up.

But that never happened. The warrior (Harry understood that his name was Bayang, the girl's Tambong) led them away from the area, deep into new rain forest, which from the position of the sun Harry estimated to lie westward, possibly southwestward. As they trekked, Harry between his captors, he was able to make out some of their conversation, which apparently they conducted only in Iban. If they spoke Iban, that was one thing, but it was quite another for Kayan to speak Iban all the time. Why did they do so? Did they suspect him of knowing their own language? Harry caught enough words from their conversation to realize they were fearful of meeting enemies on the trail. They never mentioned a meeting with the war party—or perhaps they did and he failed to understand. Harry's perplexity, coupled to his intense concentration on their words, had the beneficial effect of focusing his mind on each moment, leaving no time for brooding about the fix he was in. When they halted to eat, Harry had the odd feeling that something had happened to him during the morning's trek. Then it struck him that the fear was gone. All that ice had simply vanished, melted, leaving him sweaty in the hot jungle air and almost light-headed with joy. Yes, joy. He was alive, and clearly his captors weren't going to meet the war party and therefore had no intention of murdering him—at least not yet. So Harry reasoned while sitting cross-legged in a clearing, while his captors went on separate forays into the jungle. Soon the girl, Tambong, came back from gathering wild fruit; then the young warrior, Bayang, appeared, holding a foot-long lizard, a dart sticking from its wriggling gray body. Later, while they ate guava and chunks of lizard that the girl had boiled in a small pot taken from her knapsack, Harry opened his mouth to speak but wasn't sure what to say, so he said nothing. This happened a number of times.

At last he blurted out in broken Iban, "You name Bayang, you name Tambong. I speak little Iban." To Harry's satisfaction his captors, mouths full of lizard, were so startled that they both stood bolt upright from where they squatted by the fire.

Harry smiled for the first time in their presence. "Why Kayan speak so much Iban?" he asked pleasantly.

The reaction was more than he had bargained for. The young warrior leaped angrily to his feet, slid his parang from its scabbard, and waved it around menacingly. It took time, as it would take a great deal of time from that moment on, for Harry and his captors to communicate through Iban and gestures, but at last the white boy realized that he had incensed Bayang by calling him Kayan. Bayang was an Iban. There was probably little you could accuse him of, Harry decided grimly, that could insult him more than calling him Kayan.

So the misunderstanding was cleared up. When they headed out again, without a word Bayang slipped his anak parang between the rattan thong and Harry's wrists. It occurred to Harry that they had freed him from his bonds for one reason only: he could speak their language.

· 9 ·

Much of the whispered conversation between Bayang and Duck Foot had concerned the obat of the red-haired woman. Was she truly the Goddess of Sleep who sent dreams that could be trusted? Or was she a demon, lulling him into acceptance of dreams that would lead finally to the Land of the Dead? The answers could bring him a hero's life or his death. How to judge the truth? It was a question more suitable for dayungs than for warriors. He felt like someone entering a strange forest on a moonless night. In his confusion and puzzlement, Bayang leaned heavily on Duck Foot's opinions. Not that he would have admitted it. A warrior never told a woman that he depended on her judgment. But Bayang did, and he knew it. Only his father could have had more influence over him than this crippled girl whose affliction might well be a sign of the gods' favor. After all, the gods were mischievous; often they twisted their true intent in odd ways for nothing more than the amusement of doing it. Gods were mean, devious, willful. Everyone knew that. A warrior of worth ought to be wary in dealing with signs, omens, dreams, the gods themselves, and the underworld of demons.

Bayang was therefore cautious about trusting his own judgment when it came to things magical. This girl, sitting beneath the meditation house, had listened closely through the floorboards to the dayungs discussing obat. He was fortunate to have a person of experience with magic on this dangerous journey. Therefore, he usually followed her advice. When the girl claimed that they must learn whether the obat of the redhaired woman was good or bad, Bayang had risked his life to kidnap the white boy who would know. And yet, against Duck Foot's better judgment, he wanted to free the white boy's hands, reasoning that a bound animal was more trouble than a freed one. You had only to approach a dog when it was tied up and after it had been untied, he told her: the tied dog growled, the untied dog licked your hand. Bayang chuckled at the comparison between an English boy and a mangy longhouse dog. Duck Foot reminded him it was dangerous to laugh at anything because things had the force of gods and demons in them. You mustn't laugh at a padi of rice; if you did, you angered its gods. You mustn't injure a bush or tree without asking its forgiveness. You mustn't make fun of animals. You mustn't laugh at anything except a dog.

Bayang nodded. "As I did just now."

Duck Foot frowned at him. Dogs didn't matter to the gods, she pointed out, so by speaking of the white boy as a dog, the white boy became as worthless as a dog. "What good, then, is anything he says if he's no better than a dog?"

Chastened by her logic and therefore angry at her, Bayang had gone ahead out of spite and released the white boy. His defiance was later modified by an explanation: because the white boy spoke Iban, Bayang argued, he was worthy of Iban respect. They could talk to him and win his trust and thereafter believe what he told them.

"Talk to him," said Duck Foot. "But can you believe what he answers? Ask if the obat is a goddess. If he says yes, can you believe him? If he says no, can you believe him? How can you decide when to believe him?"

Bayang nodded glumly. "We'll move from place to place till we know."

He found himself respecting Duck Foot more and liking her less. At the longhouse he had grown accustomed to watching girls weaving baskets and feeding the livestock and cooking and washing, but until now he'd never treated one as his equal. When they set out, he'd simply expected Duck Foot to do what she was told. From the outset he had meant to treat her better than his friends might have done. He had even given her permission to ask questions without asking first if she could ask. He had done this to put her at ease. Perhaps he had gone too far. She no longer asked permission to say things, and often volunteered her opinion without his wanting it. When she didn't agree with him, she frowned darkly. And to make matters worse, his surprise at her boldness was compounded by his need for her advice.

Looking at the white boy—they knew him now as Harry—Bayang wondered if Harry found white girls mystifying. Sometimes, in glancing sideways at the round forehead and large black eyes of the girl, Bayang suspected no demon in the forest was any stranger than Tambong.

They wandered in a southwesterly direction, awaiting signs and omens. Although Harry marched as a prisoner between the Iban, he was allowed to carry a hardwood stave to help him navigate in the scarcely discernible footpaths that had been hacked out of this jungle in some forgotten past: one, two, maybe five years ago.

It was after a brief downpour. Through the musically rhythmic dripping of raindrops on fronds the size of drumheads, Bayang heard a single grunting sound.

That was enough for him.

Instantly he slipped through a tangle of undergrowth, his chest parallel to the ground, one hand holding the blowgun parallel to it as well. He lifted each foot high and put it down evenly, distributing his weight on leaves in such fashion that they didn't crackle, as if he had cushions of air under his callused soles.

Another grunting sound.

Bayang halted to sniff the air. He turned his head while inhaling the perfume of orchids, the loamy odor of decaying roots and leaves, until a pungent new smell broke through theirs and gave him a direction. Before going farther, he reached with one hand over his shoulder, located the end of a dart in his quiver, took it out and spun it rapidly in his fingers, this whirling motion tightening the cotton around its shaft. From his rattan belt he took a small pouch that contained a paste made from ipoh-tree sap. He rubbed the sticky poison on the sharp tip of the dart, which he then slipped by its blunt end into the blowgun. He held the seven-foot shaft in both hands near its mouthpiece of monkey bone.

After another sniff, he moved forward in his slow, methodical, high-stepping way until ahead, through the leaves, he saw something brown, like a large pile of earth, on the jungle floor. Now he could hear the steady guttural breathing. A few more steps and he could clearly see what he had been stalking: a full-grown wild pig was lying in a muddy water hole, cooling off. Clouds of flies formed a kind of diaphanous veil around the creature's tiny pink ears, bloodshot eyes, and curved yellow tusks. Its front hooves, extended straight ahead, gave it a child-ish look, as if the big muddy animal were teasing an invisible playmate in a game of tag.

Slowly, carefully, his upper body still bent parallel to the ground, Bayang lifted the blowgun to his mouth, gripping the mouthpiece firmly in both hands. When he took a quick fierce inhale, the sound was different from those expected by the lolling pig. The creature had just enough time to turn its long snout sideways and stare from its little eyes in Bayang's direction before the dart entered his body just back of the left front leg, in the region of the heart. Lurching to its feet, the pig snorted and tried ineffectually to turn its snout enough to root out the sliver of wood that had sunk halfway into its flesh. Then the pig took off, scampering with astonishing speed out of the mudhole and into the surrounding foliage. It guided its bulk among thornbushes and knobby roots with amazing skill and lightness, the little hooves thudding rapidly through the undergrowth.

Bayang followed at a leisurely trot, now holding the blowgun upright. There was no need to hurry. All he must do was keep the crashing sound within hearing distance. After a while the sound of thrashing would grow weaker, at intervals farther apart, until it ceased altogether. It was not necessary for him to turn and wait for Duck Foot, who would be following his tracks at her own pace. Reaching the animal at last, he'd squat nearby and let the poison continue its work until there was no more danger from the weakened pig's tusks. Then he'd go in.

When Bayang suddenly left the trail and plunged into undergrowth, Duck Foot knew he was on the scent of something to eat, so she followed his tracks without trying to catch up. Leading the way for her captive, she turned now and then to wave him onward. Duck Foot felt uneasy alone in the white boy's presence. Nothing had yet given her assurance that the redheaded, pale-skinned Harry was human. Only one thing about him was certain: he wanted the obat now hanging from Bayang's neck. Duck Foot had caught him staring at it with longing, as if nothing in the world meant as much to him as having it back. Such longing was always the result of powerful magic. What would he do with the obat if they gave it to him? Perhaps he'd turn them both into lizards or transport them through the air to the mountain above the Land of the Dead or put tiny crabs in their guts or cause them to go blind. Anything was possible if the obat was strong enough and placed in the hands of an evil spirit.

Such gloomy, fearful thoughts were still with Duck Foot when she reached a clearing where Bayang squatted to one side, calmly smoking a cheroot, and the pig lay on its belly not six feet away, breathing heavily. Duck Foot squatted and motioned for the white boy to do the same. Finally the pig began wheezing, then intermittently gave a little squeal, while its breath came in short rapid gusts.

Bayang took a long puff from the cheroot, laid it down on a leaf, and rose to his feet while pulling out the parang from its liana-vine-wrapped scabbard. Walking up to the gasping animal, he bent over and with one long, expert motion slit its throat. Blood spurted out in hot jets that filled the clearing with a robust animal smell. The jungle became abruptly silent. The curved yellow tusks as long as Bayang's thumb protruded farther from the animal's lips, and the wiry bristles of its snout twitched a few times violently, then became still.

Duck Foot was observing the white boy; what she saw was encouraging: Harry looked stricken—his face deathly pale, his eyes round and wide, his mouth set grimly. It occurred to her that the death of the pig was troubling him. Would a demon be troubled by any death? None that she had ever heard of. Perhaps Harry really was a human, if plainly a weak and cowardly one. This possibility made her smile with relief. When Harry turned to look at her and caught her smiling, his expression changed from horror to surprise. This also comforted Duck Foot, because he seemed defenseless again, as he'd first looked to her while coming naked, pale, and frightened from the pond.

When Bayang waved to her, Duck Foot got up and went to work. First she gathered fern leaves, broad and feathery ones, and formed them into a wide bed upon which, with Bayang's help, she dragged the big carcass of the pig. Here Bayang skinned the beast with his small-bladed anak parang, then cut out the tastiest morsels, such as the liver, the tongue, and the muscles inside the lower rib cage, along with cubed pieces of belly meat and entrail, which Duck Foot skewered on hardwood stakes. After he'd bashed the skull in with a rock, she wrapped the brains in a palm frond.

While Harry sat there gawking, they collected wood. Bayang split some for kindling and used the rest to build a fire and a rack above it. Duck Foot went in search of wild ginger, which she found nearby in abundance and crushed in the mortar of a coconut shell, then mixed with salt and chilies from her knapsack. After Bayang had started the fire with his flint, Duck Foot placed the wrapped brains on a makeshift frame of vertebrae hacked out of the corpse. She put the brains to steam on top of the rack alongside the skewered cubes of meat. While that cooked, Duck Foot prepared another dish from sago flour she had brought along. She moistened it in gouts of pig blood, threw the wet mass into her little cast-iron pot, added more blood, and heated it all to boiling.

She smiled happily at Bayang. They were going to have a feast, all the more welcome because she was nearly sure now that they were traveling with a human—one so weak he grew pale at the sight of blood.

He had to admit the roast pig was delicious, though he refused the steamed brains and the sago flour boiled in blood and a smoking portion of entrail. His back against a tree trunk, Harry watched his captors bolt their food ravenously. Camp flies hovered around the bloody mess of sago that they stuffed into their mouths. At times their fingers were thick from swarms of painted flies, which they brushed off casually and which returned just as casually a few seconds later: waves of insects alighting and crawling along thumbs, wrists, blood-soaked palms.

Harry was repelled by the way they ate. Worse, they were thieves. Every time he stared at the locket around Bayang's neck—this was often—Harry wanted to rip it off and strike the Iban full across the mouth. In physical strength he felt more than a match for the wiry native. Nor did he like the girl. Heretofore she had regarded him with a kind of fearful wariness; now she smirked from her broad mouth, as if amused by him. Whereas Bayang seemed merely indifferent to his presence, Harry felt that the girl held him in contempt. If he came to harm, most likely it would be because of her. From what Harry could make of their conversation, the young warrior usually followed her advice. Would it help to smile at her? Harry thought better of it. She might take it for weakness. Being crippled had probably given her uncommon strength of mind and will. She'd turn on him without warning if he seemed to lack courage. He resolved to meet her hard gaze with a bold stare of his own.

By the time his captors had gorged themselves, it was dusk. Clearly there would be no more traveling today. Both of the Iban lay back against tree trunks, their stomachs greatly distended, as they belched and sighed and struggled to find positions of comfort for their bloated stomachs.

It was nearly dark before the girl stirred and got to her feet. Reaching up into the crotch of a tree, she pulled down something that looked to Harry at first like a bundle of rags. Actually it was part of a termite nest. She parceled out bits of it in a wide circle and stepped inside, motioning for Harry to do the same. He obeyed. The girl seemed more relaxed with him than before, perhaps because she had eaten to satiety. Making a motion with one arm, she imitated with great skill the slithering motion of a snake, then pointed beyond the circle of scattered termite nest.

It was clear to Harry that the material from the termite nest was a means of keeping snakes away. With a grimace the girl sniffed hard. So snakes disliked the smell of termites. Lying down within the circle, Harry curled up on his side in the fern leaves stinking of dead pig. There was hardly time for him to notice the moon as it shone down on the clearing. He fell at once into a profound sleep.

And he awoke with a start.

There was a faint glow in the sky. It was dawn. Glancing around, he saw that his captors were lying in the same positions as the night before. They were sleeping off the effects of a remarkable gluttony.

If ever he had a chance to escape, it was now, Harry told himself. Trembling with sudden excitement, he sat upright, then without hesitation rose to his feet and stepped beyond the circle of termite nest. For an instant he thought of the locket, but if he tried to remove it from Bayang's neck, surely the Iban would awaken. Picking up his hardwood stave, Harry thought of attacking his captors. He could either smash them in the head or stab them in the heart.

Instead, he slipped out of the clearing and tried to retrace the route taken by Tambong yesterday. Jungle was coming out of the darkness like something rising from the sea: leaf, trunk, vine, emerging from the subterranean depths of the night. A ground mist flowed around his hesitant feet as they stumbled across roots in the attempt to follow a path that might be a path only in his imagination. Brushing against giant ferns, he was showered with cold sprays of dew. Patches of yellow phosphorescence, clinging to tree trunks, glowed eerily until the shimmering blue of early day pervaded the jungle.

He traveled until sunlight appeared through leafy branches before halting for a rest. They would have caught up with him by now if they were following. The Iban must still be lying there, bloated and stunned by their feasting. They might not awaken for hours, and by then, once he reached a stream, he'd be free, because they wouldn't be able to follow his track through water. Harry felt both elated and afraid. He was truly alone now. He was like a cork bobbing on the vast expanse of a great ocean. Which way should he take? The coast lay to the northwest; that way lay whatever civilization there was in Borneo. He'd be able to find that general direction by watching the angle of the sunlight coming through the trees.

The sun seemed to be halfway up the eastern sky before he reached a small river. It was very shallow, so that rocks dotted its bubbling surface like myriad little islands. He stepped into the stream, slipping and sliding but managing to keep his balance along its course. He persisted in this difficult way for a long time, falling three times and scraping his knee, his elbow. Finally, exhausted and hungry, he stumbled out of the stream and sat panting on the bank. Iridescent dragonflies hovered around his face, while a mouse deer on the opposite bank regarded him warily as it lowered its slim, delicate snout to the water for a drink. A vine of blue morning glories twisted around the nearby trunk of a rain tree. He looked at the mouse deer, at the morning glories, at the hovering dragonflies, and for a few wonderful moments Harry Windsor felt utterly at one with the jungle. Not until now had he fully appreciated its beauty, its serenity, its timelessness. He felt as though he'd crawled into its heart and his own heart beat to the same rhythm. Lying back, blinking in the sunlight, he was at peace with this world, so much at peace that he was certain nothing in it could really harm him. He had learned the secret of the jungle. He was as much a part of it as any native.

Getting to his feet, Harry moved with a light foot into the undergrowth, preparing for another trek through the rain forest. He had not gone far, however, before his need for something to eat became overwhelming. Uncle Julian had once told him that the rule of the jungle was to eat anything the animals eat. If animals didn't eat it, you mustn't either.

Fine. But what did the animals eat?

He decided to wait. But while Harry continued to struggle with vines and thornbushes and root systems, his step was no longer buoyant. Soon he could think of nothing but his hunger. Then, to his surprise and relief, he came upon a stand of large trees which he recognized to be a kind of rattan. With the Iban he had eaten the mealy inside of rattan trunk; it had tasted no worse than the morning porridge served in his boarding school. But he had no knife to cut into a trunk—his had been taken by the Iban. Searching around, he finally discovered a trunk already split by the tension of another tree growing across it. The yellow marrow inside was exposed. He tried to pick it out, but the fiber was tough, so he had to use his stave to dig some free.

Harry was lifting a small mouthful to his lips when he heard a little thud. Looking to one side at the rattan trunk, he saw a dart, its end quivering slightly. Leaping up, he turned to face Bayang, who held the blowgun up as if to shoot again. Tambong scooted forward and grabbed the fibrous marrow out of Harry's hand. Harry realized then that Bayang hadn't been trying to shoot him, only to startle him. So they had easily followed his track. Crestfallen, Harry backed against the tree and stood there, waiting for them to tie his wrists with a rattan thong again.

Instead, Bayang put down the blowgun and walked up to the split tree. With his anak parang he cut out some of the mealy substance and pretended to eat it, swallowing hard afterward and then gripping his throat. He acted out the horror of strangling, with his cupped hand moving out from his throat as if the flesh were expanding beneath his fingers. Falling down, Bayang gasped for breath, his eyes rolled dramatically, and at last he groaned and lay back as if dead.

Tambong said, "Mato tagaro," nodding emphatically.

Harry understood perfectly. The marrow of this particular rattan, the mato tagaro, expanded when you swallowed it, your throat swelling until you strangled to death. They had saved him from a horrible fate.

Bayang motioned.

Harry got docilely between his captors. They led him away from the tree of death.

· 10 ·

That night, after Harry fell asleep, Bayang rose to his feet, held up one finger to command silence, and led Duck Foot from the clearing down to a stream, where they squatted on the moonlit bank for a talk.

Bayang expressed the baleful opinion that the white boy was too ignorant to last in the jungle. They couldn't watch him every moment. Sooner or later he'd be killed somehow by a plant or an animal or his own clumsiness.

Duck Foot agreed. Then, too, she added, there was always a chance of the Kayan discovering them, because everywhere he went in the forest Harry left the heavy-footed tracks of a dozen wild boars; if the Kayan attacked them, they might have to leave him behind or give up three heads instead of one.

"We could take him to the longhouse," Bayang suggested.

After a thoughtful silence, Duck Foot disagreed. "If we do, your father will send him back to the English. The Iban aren't at war now. They'll sacrifice your dream for peace."

"We can't go home. We'll keep wandering till its meaning is clear . . ." Bayang fingered the locket hanging around his neck. "Tomorrow I ask him."

"Yes, ask. He's not an evil spirit. An evil spirit loves blood, but Harry doesn't, he hates it. What he tells us we can believe."

"Tomorrow we know what he knows."

"What then?" Duck Foot asked. "What do we do with him?"

Bayang had already thought of that, so his answer was ready. "We let him come with us wherever we go in search of the Big Fish."

"But if he slows us down or gets hurt?"

"We go our own way."

"That means he won't be with us long."

Bayang shrugged. "We won't take his head, but we won't let him keep us from finding the Big Fish."

"If you think that way, we'll find it," Duck Foot declared happily, relieved that Bayang was showing the ironwood-hard strength of a great warrior.

Next morning they finished the last of the pig; it was already somewhat gamy and by noon, in such heat, it would be utterly spoiled. Duck Foot had gathered a potful of paku kubok—wild vegetables—which she cooked with sago flour. While the mess boiled, Bayang squatted nearby and watched a chic-chac lizard as it stalked a black fly. The lizard eased forward almost imperceptibly, while the fly busied itself at the heart of a rotting mango. Suddenly the chic-chac's tongue flicked out, the fly instantly vanished, the throat of the lizard swelled, and its translucent buff-colored body turned a rich brown as the insect slid into its crop.

"Harry," Bayang said, turning to the white boy, who had just finished his portion of the pig and was wiping his greasy hands on a leaf. Bayang lifted the locket in his right hand, twisting it on its chain before releasing the clasp and letting the locket snap open like two halves of a shell. "What?" Noting that Harry stared hard at the red-haired woman, Bayang tapped the portrait with his forefinger and repeated the question. "What?"

Harry seemed to be searching for words in Iban to say something, but his grimacing proved that he couldn't find them. So he simply pointed to the portrait, then to himself. Bayang glanced at Duck Foot, who offered no opinion.

"What?" Bayang asked again impatiently.

Harry made a cradle of his arms and rocked them back and forth, then pointed again to the locket.

"Harry's mother," Duck Foot declared.

Raising his eyebrows, Bayang asked her if she believed it. She did, Duck Foot acknowledged, but she was frowning.

"You believe it, but what else do you believe?" Bayang asked her.

"I remember a dayung talking of a goddess who had hair the color of fire. I think this mother of Harry is a goddess."

"Then is he a god?"

Duck Foot shook her head. "His hair is not so red. He might be the child of a goddess and still be human. I'm sure he's no god. We needn't fear him, but if I'm right and she's a goddess, we must fear her. Ask him if she comes into his dreams."

It took Bayang a long time to convey this question. He acted out sleeping, then having good dreams by curling up with a smile on his face and nightmares by twisting around violently. At last Harry understood that dreams were meant, but he didn't think of them in relation to his mother. The sun was high over the clearing before he finally caught on. Harry tapped his forehead hard as if acknowledging his slowness.

"Yes," he said then in English, smiling. "I dream of my mother. Yes," he said in Iban, nodding vigorously. With his right hand he pointed to the locket, then, with eyes closed, to his head and heart.

"She comes to him in dreams," affirmed Duck Foot.

Bayang leaned tensely toward the girl. "Will she come to me in my dreams?"

"If she's the Goddess of Sleep—and I believe she is—she can come into the dreams of anyone."

Bayang clutched the locket possessively, snapping it shut. "Then with this I can dream the dreams that lead to the Big Fish."

Duck Foot was staring at the white boy, whose gaze never left the locket. "I don't think we can trust him anymore. He knows you need the obat of his mother, but he wants it for himself. One of us must stay awake at night and watch him, or he might kill us for the obat."

Bayang saw the good sense in that, and added for good measure, "If he gets in the way of my dreaming, I will kill him."

"Yes," said Duck Foot. "You must let nothing stand in the way."

This was a day for animals.

They saw water buffalo, crocodiles, a rainbow of parakeets sitting on a single branch, a large pack of noisy gibbons, wood partridges, bird-eating spiders, otters sporting in a narrow river, the large chock-wah lizard that won't run from humans. They even saw a clouded leopard skulking through the undergrowth: its flanks an earthy brown color, with the insides of its legs pure white and with a thickset spotted head and two broad black bands running from its upright little ears to its sinuous shoulders. Bayang watched it slink away. The Kayan valued this rare kind of leopard beyond all other animals. They used its teeth for marriage necklaces and its pelts for the war coats of headmen. The thought of the Kayan sobered him a moment, but his general mood was buoyant and optimistic, as he frequently touched the obat around his neck.

He let himself dream while awake, and in this trancelike state began to fashion a great dream of the future so real that it seemed to have already happened. He built a new longhouse for his people. It had sixty family doors and was supported on ironwood posts able to withstand both weather and insects for a hundred years. He buried charms in the holes made for these posts, and after the posts were erected, he imposed a taboo on eating sour fruits until the longhouse was completed. It took a year. Just before the full moon his people moved from the old longhouse to the new one. There were many days of feasting and visits in decorated boats by neighboring tribesmen who debarked to the sound of the kangkuang, a huge wooden drum carved especially for the occasion. There was eating, drinking, dancing until dawn, and then three years later a final celebration at which all taboos in the longhouse were lifted. For two years prior to the feast of Memasi So, everyone worked hard to provide sacrificial bulls and expensive glutinous rice and sweet cakes. He, Bayang, oversaw it all as the headman of the longhouse.

This fantasy remained with Bayang all day and night, even following him into sleep and his entrance into the Dream World. Walking down an unfamiliar footpath, abruptly he stepped on a tortoise, the animal of death. Stumbling on its shell, he crashed into a dead tree around which two snakes were entwined, hissing at each other, baring their fangs. He watched them until one bit the other in the neck, drawing a geyser of black blood. He shook from fear, because few sights were as evil as that of snakes fighting. Turning and fleeing, he lunged through the dense rain forest without knowing which way to go. Then Bayang realized he was utterly lost. As he wandered hopelessly through the shadows, the overhead sun burst through the branches with a light so brilliant that he couldn't keep his eyes open, but the sunshine burned white-hot through the lids, boring into his mind until Bayang awoke in a cold sweat, panting, horrified.

He did not wait for morning, but crawled over and shook

Duck Foot awake. In rapid whispers he related the dream, and to his dismay the girl concurred: the tortoise, the entwined snakes, the bite that drew blood, getting lost in the jungle, enduring the hot light of the sun were all signs of evil. His nightmare was as terrible as a nightmare could be.

Duck Foot got up and left the clearing, getting far beyond earshot of Harry, who might be faking sleep. Bayang followed behind her, until the limping girl stopped at the bank of a stream and turned to him.

"She sent you the dream," Duck Foot maintained, reaching out and touching the locket.

"Does it mean my death?"

"It means we can't cause his. The mother protects her son. She warns you to look after Harry. She is the sunlight coming through the shadows. She can see everything in the jungle. We can't leave him along the trail, and we can't stop him from doing anything he wants, even if it's harmful to us. We must protect him as she would or you're lost in the jungle forever."

Opening the locket, Bayang squinted in the moonlight at the smiling, rather square face of a woman whose eyes in this gloom were two holes like a ghost's. "The future, everything," he murmured before snapping it shut, "is here. So I will do anything he wants except give this back to him."

In the morning Bayang ordered Duck Foot to make Harry a good meal. While she gathered paku kubok, he went into the forest and shot down a plantain squirrel, which he skinned on the spot. He was thinking of his talk with Duck Foot last night. They had no choice but to obey the Goddess of Sleep and take good care of her son. Then he gutted the squirrel and tossed the entrails across a nest of elephant ants, a few dozen of which instantly formed a defensive ring round the entrance, their big mandibles spread wide, ready to attack whatever had disturbed the tranquillity of the nest.

Before getting back to camp, Bayang halted at the sound of a familiar birdcall: a long fluid *ko-ah ko-ah ko-ah* that changed abruptly into a rapid percussive *kum! kum! kum!*

It was the call of the scarlet-rumped trogon. Glancing around at the trees, Bayang finally located the bird tilting on a branch midway up in the forest canopy: a stout, hooked yellow bill; a square-cut crimson tail with a black band around it; a dark green chest and back. The trogon's call was a good-luck call. If you heard it while deciding something, you made the right decision. Bayang breathed a sigh of relief. This omen confirmed their interpretation of the dream.

When he returned to camp and gave the squirrel to Duck Foot for roasting, he fussed over a bewildered Harry, who looked plainly frightened by so much attention—Bayang squatting beside him, patting his arm, his belly, asking in Iban if he felt good, if he was hungry, if he wanted more rest.

Finished eating, Bayang insisted on Duck Foot's going out and finding a certain vine; after being pounded and dipped in water, it could be kneaded into the skin of legs and ankles to keep leeches away. With his own hands he applied the mixture to Harry's legs. He also insisted on Duck Foot's halting along the path to collect obat ular, a jungle creeper, used for snakebite. That evening she pounded it into a pulp and saved it in case they needed such medicine.

"Today," Bayang told her, "I saw a banded krait not two feet away from Harry. Of course, he didn't see it, and I didn't tell him it was there for fear he might jump and the snake strike. We must be prepared for this fool to be bitten by a krait, a viper, a cobra—anything."

Bayang's vigilance and solicitude were so intense that he couldn't maintain them for long. After two days he quieted down—to the relief of both Duck Foot and Harry—though he did keep a close parental eye on the white boy. The Goddess of Sleep had been very clear: her son must be protected from harm in the jungle.

And so they continued to meander along, heading generally toward the southwest, which would bring them close to the longhouse if not actually there. They were waiting for further signs, especially those which came in dreams. There was nothing to do but hike and eat and wait for nightfall, when it was proper for Bayang to enter the Dream World.

For three nights running he had no dreams worth remembering. That in itself, according to Duck Foot, proved they were right in protecting the boy. Had this been a wrong interpretation, surely another dream would have told Bayang so. All they could do now was travel and wait. It was like the forest itself awaiting rain: animal and plant could do nothing but hang on until the hoped-for downpour arrived. You could not rush a dream, either favorable or unfavorable. Even a young warrior like Bayang, Duck Foot told him, was helpless when entering the Dream World.

Yet they both felt a new urgency in their search for the Big Fish. Harry was the reason for it. Each day he learned a little more Iban and was becoming adept, too, at gesturing, so he was able to communicate better. Moreover, their obvious desire to make him happy encouraged in him a new boldness. He asked where they were going. He wanted to know why they were bringing him along. He promised to give them a reward for taking him back to Kuching.

Then he asked for the locket.

Shaking his head furiously, Bayang gripped the shaft of his blowgun so hard that the dark knuckles of his hand turned an ivory color.

Through gestures and labored Iban, the white boy then asked why the locket was so valuable to them when he could give them ten times its worth in gold if they returned it and took him back to Kuching.

"Please give me the locket," Harry said in both English and broken Iban.

"Aahkit," Bayang repeated, holding it tightly between thumb and forefinger. He jabbed his own chest sharply to indicate that the aahkit was his.

That night, his jaw set grimly, Bayang whispered to Duck Foot as they squatted alongside a mosquito-infested pond, "If the goddess didn't care, I would kill him now."

"Yes, and you should. But the goddess does care. If he dies, I think we all die."

·11·

Each night when Bayang fell asleep now he dreamed, but never vividly enough to remember the dream later. Like any Iban denied the memory of dreams, he felt starved, restless, filled with a craving of the soul for nourishment. Was the Goddess of Sleep punishing him because he wanted to kill her son?

He went to Duck Foot with that question, having come to depend on her judgment, which seemed more useful the longer they remained in the jungle among spirits that favored her.

They had climbed to the top of a hill for their talk. If Harry wanted to overhear them, he'd have to climb it, too, and they'd see him before he reached them. It was Duck Foot's idea to come up here. For a long time she thought about Bayang's question.

Waiting for her response, he noticed to his dismay a limb suddenly fell from a tree. There wasn't the slightest stir of breeze that might have caused it. When a branch fell without reason, most probably an evil spirit had brushed against it. He was surrounded by evil spirits, while his own spirit languished as if dying of hunger.

"You're right," Duck Foot finally declared. "The Goddess of Sleep is punishing you for wanting her son dead. You're starving to death. Stay here."

She returned to their camp below the hill, where Harry was dozing. Does he dream, Duck Foot wondered idly, as she got her small iron pot and knapsack. Does he have more than one spirit in him the way we do?

Returning to Bayang, she made a fire, fetched water from a nearby stream, and boiled a handful of rice from her knapsack.

"This is spirit rice," she declared. Before leaving the longhouse, Duck Foot then confessed, she had stolen some of this special rice from the dayung's meditation house.

Bayang was shocked. Spirit rice was kept only by the dayung, who dispensed a few grains on feast days. It was called spirit rice because a small portion of the padi had been fertilized by the spirit of a dead man. When a man died, he lay within a wooden coffin in a grave house away from the main building. A number of tubular reeds attached to the corpse emerged from holes drilled in the coffin. Through these reeds passed liquids of decomposition into glazed ceramic jars that stood around the coffin. In weeks and months, as the body became dry bones, so the spirit, detached from it, became purer. Once the liquids were collected in jars, they were poured by the dayung onto a section of the padi, enriching it with the dead man's spirit, which entered the growing kernels of rice. When this special rice was harvested and a man ate it, he also ate spirit. Aside from that given out on feast days, this precious rice was used only to help sick people get well. Its use was determined solely by the dayung.

"While eating," Duck Foot told Bayang, spreading out a few dozen grains on a leaf, "think of the spirit in it. You must think of the spirit or it won't enter you. I've heard the dayung say you can eat a pile of such rice and it does nothing unless you think of the spirit within."

Bayang took up each grain of rice between thumb and fore-finger. He stared at each brown pellet, put it in his mouth, and chewed slowly with eyes closed. He imagined a man of his father's size and figure lying in a wooden coffin in a grave house. He thought of the corpse rotting; and as it rotted, the entrails, flesh, and gristle became liquid and this liquid was spirit. Drop by drop the spirit dripped through the reed tubes down into the glazed jars and then was poured from the jars into the padi. Bayang thought of this process of decomposition until nothing existed in his mind except the imagined idea of a rice shoot, having absorbed the liquid remains of a dead man, growing tall on the strength of a human spirit.

What he ate now was the spirit of someone who had once lived in his own longhouse.

It must have taken him a long, long time before every grain of rice was consumed, because the sun had nearly set when finally Bayang opened his eyes.

Duck Foot squatted nearby, having watched him swallow each grain. She nodded approvingly. "You're no longer starved. I see it in your face. There's new spirit there."

Bayang stared at the girl, still amazed by her boldness. No one else in the longhouse would have dared to steal spirit rice from the dayung. Yet Bayang realized that without this infusion of spirit, he might have wasted away as people did from hacking coughs or stomach pains, except that he would have died of spiritual hunger—the most horrible of maladies.

Bayang believed that he owed her his life.

Harry felt that they were plotting to kill him, that in fact they had intended to kill him all along but for some reason had kept putting it off. A few days ago, when they suddenly became solicitous of his comfort and happiness, he'd been sure it was a prelude to slitting his throat. Everything they did either frightened or disgusted him—the way they treated him with disdain; the way they killed animals, with a kind of casual indifference; and the way they consumed what they killed, with no apparent distaste for parts considered inedible by civilized people; the way they heeded sights and sounds that meant nothing whatsoever to himself.

Of the two Iban, he feared the girl, Tambong, more. She had regular features and large, pretty eyes, but the expression in them was cold, and at times, when he caught her glancing sideways at him, murderous. They narrowed as if she were estimating when to run her anak parang into his back. Harry suffered greatly during their treks, knowing she was but a step behind him. His back was as vulnerable as the belly of an overthrown turtle. How often he wished to lunge off the path and escape!

His experience with the deadly species of rattan, however, had taught Harry a lesson. Though he feared the Iban, his greater fear was of being alone in this vast, unpredictable jungle. The ocean he'd crossed to get from England to Borneo had impressed him by its size and majesty, but it was nothing compared to the jungle, which seemed like a live, intelligent thing, capable of conscious evil. It made him feel as though he were being watched by a presence that held an instantaneous power of life and death over him. Sometimes at night, when the Iban slept, he awoke suddenly into an immense silence broken at times by troops of bats swooping out of their inverted-umbrella positions on the lower side of tree limbs, leaving in the night air a pungent odor like burnt leather as they took flight and went hunting. He imagined them hunting, their high shrieks guiding them toward the warm, throbbing bodies of tiny rodents in the bush.

In the endless darkness of such nights he thought of unhappy things. His uncle had told him, for example, of the

Bornean shrike, an ashy-black and crimson bird that never hesitated to kill its companion if the latter was wounded or sick. He kept thinking of the shrike. What made it do such a callous thing? Why did humans fight wars and torture one another? Then he wondered if his uncle was still alive, if any of the expedition had survived the Kayan attack. Had he himself been spared merely to suffer longer? What was this life?

Harry recalled his childhood in growing realization of how good it had been. Until his parents died, he'd enjoyed the best of things. And after losing his parents, he'd absorbed the grief, taken heart, and gone on. But out there in the jungle he felt there was nothing to hold on to. That was how he thought of it: nothing to grasp, nothing solid, nothing that might give him a sense of order and continuity. He was like a cork bobbing on a vast surface of shifting greenery and sunlight.

Then there was the question of how much longer he might live. When would they finally decide to kill him? He had only a stave to protect himself with. The thought of it, however, stiffened his will. They'd not have an easy time of murdering him. He'd fight back. He'd show them that an Englishman, no matter how unskilled in the rain forest, could stand up when the going got rough. He'd give them a scare before succumbing to poisoned darts. He'd go down honorably like a Windsor.

Soon an odd and terrible fantasy created itself in his mind, while hour followed hour on the hot, humid trails of the rain forest. In this fantasy he'd received two darts, one near the heart, and the chill ascending his arms and legs was the chill of a poison-induced death. But he'd fought hard—given Bayang some telling blows—and as he lay on the leafy floor of the jungle, looking up at their barbaric faces, he asked them, please, for the aahkit to hold in his hands until he breathed his last—then they could take back his mother's portrait for what-ever savage ritual they had in mind. Out of respect for his bravery, Bayang placed it in his hands, which slowly but surely grew cold against the round metal, so that his last memory on earth was of his hands clasping the locket tightly.

Harry tried to shake off the fantasy. He understood it did nothing except deprive him of a sense of what was really happening. To his credit—Harry understood it was to his credit—he shed the fantasy the way a snake sheds an old skin, and he awoke to the possibility of somehow staying alive. Why? Harry didn't know, but he became increasingly conscious of watching his captors for signs that instead of wanting him dead they really wanted him to live. He felt they all wanted to live, and such extended existence depended on their being alive together. It was an odd idea, but then, since joining them in the rain forest, whatever was odd soon became commonplace. He started to talk more, make requests, tempt them to get him back to Kuching. Even when he asked for the aahkit and got from Bayang a menacing shake of the blowgun, Harry saw a glimmer of hope, like a tiny thread of sunlight wriggling inside a network of deep shadows.

Then came the anteater.

Harry smelled it long before seeing it: an offensive odor seemed to descend upon the jungle, blanketing tree and bush with the smell of swamp rot. Then, following the Iban, who crouched and padded forward slowly, Harry saw it at last. The thing seemed to be a ball of plated metal lying on the ground, and streams of black ants were flowing onto it, seeking entrance among the hard scales that covered its body. Harry figured the stench came from the creature because it was dead, but after a few minutes, when hundreds of ants had slipped under the hard plates, the anteater uncurled suddenly and got to its feet, flexing its long sharp claws that could tear an ant or termite nest to bits within minutes. Somehow it tightened its scales so the ants within could not escape.

Harry looked at the Iban, expecting Bayang to attack the animal. But earlier that day they had bagged two lemurs, so there was no need for taking more meat. They simply watched what the anteater did.

It waddled toward a nearby pond, entered, and slid under the water. When it came to the surface, Harry could see the scales rise on its back and open out so that clumps of ants emerged. With its long, sticky tongue the anteater licked up scores of the insects that were blackening the pond.

Harry turned instinctively and was startled to see Duck Foot smiling at him. Why? he wondered fearfully, until it occurred to him that the Iban had enjoyed the anteater's performance, too. He smiled back. The Iban and Harry smiled then at the anteater. Having shammed death, the creature had tempted the ants by exposing its flesh, trapped them, and obtained a hearty meal.

Harry understood now why he felt the jungle was a live intelligent thing: it was made up of live intelligent things. He felt a profound new respect for the jungle; a scaly anteater had taught it to him.

Toward noon Harry was distracted by the heavy, angry-sounding leap of silver leaf monkeys through the treetops, so he nearly bumped into Bayang, who had stopped abruptly on the trail to look at something.

Harry leaned forward, too, and squinted at a few strands of fur stuck to a thornbush. He couldn't identify what they'd come from, these pale tawny threads with spots of black on them, but Bayang could. The Iban growled and made claws of his hands, which Harry took to mean a big cat. A clouded leopard?

"Kayan," Bayang said. He made the motion of putting on a jacket of some sort, then pretended to be stalking something, after which he jumped around and waved his hand back and forth as if wielding a knife.

At last Harry got it: these strands came from a Kayan war coat of clouded leopard fur.

Bayang curled his fingers and moved them rapidly until Harry understood that the Iban wanted his stick. Harry gave it to him, then watched as the Iban took out his parang and quickly, skillfully, sharpened one end to a point, making of the stick a spear.

He handed it back to Harry without a word.

So Kayan were in the neighborhood.

If they were attacked, Harry wondered, would he run in panic as he'd done last time? Father used to say you could be a coward in battle once, but once was all you got. Harry remembered this remark so vividly that he could see his father's broad florid face, the luxuriant mustache, the cool blue eyes.

· 12 ·

H arry had just seen a green-and-black butterfly as big as his hand, when ahead of him Bayang suddenly vanished. Vanished. Like a puff of smoke.

This happened so abruptly that Harry halted before realizing that he'd better leap off the trail, too. And then he was flailing in undergrowth, stumbling over roots, following the quiver of fronds left in the Iban's wake. Harry was so precipitous in his flight that he nearly fell on Bayang, who was crouching alongside the trunk of a rain tree. The Iban had his parang drawn. Nearby squatted Duck Foot. How had she got here, too? Harry wondered for an instant, but then there wasn't time for wondering, because both Iban were setting out again and he was following them, mechanically, blindly.

At a whoop that sounded like a gibbon's, Bayang froze, one foot raised off the ground. Harry didn't have to be told that the whoop hadn't come from a gibbon. He tried to quiet the rattling sound of his own breathing. Could the Kayan stalking them hear his heart pounding? He felt ashamed of it. Then they were going forward again through the dense foliage.

For Harry, this plunge through the jungle seemed endless, and he was gasping for air when they emerged onto the bank of a small river.

Without hesitation, Bayang waded in waist-deep, with the girl and Harry following. As he twisted and weaved to get through the swirling water, Harry saw, from the corner of his eye, a white-bellied eagle glide lazily over the jungle canopy. How could anything, Harry wondered, go about its daily business when *this* was happening?

Sloshing out of the river onto the opposite bank, he had just enough time to see Bayang disappear into a stand of giant bamboo. Then he was in there himself and beyond the bamboo into a hardwood forest. Leaf-heavy branches blocked out the sun, leaving the jungle floor in an eerie light. Harry felt underwater for a moment, disoriented. Then a whooshing sound came from the bushes to his right. He stared at a dart sunk half its length into a tree trunk ahead. It was in reaching distance as he stumbled past and lurched into a run.

The Kayan were shooting at him.

His back was exposed, making him as vulnerable as an overturned turtle!

Harry turned, gripping his stave in its middle. Visible through the foliage behind him, a man was trotting along, blowgun in one hand, parang in the other. Twisted brass rings in his distended earlobes were swaying from the motion of his rhythmic running.

Harry tightened his grip on the stick. If the Kayan stops to load the blowgun, I'll run, Harry decided. If he keeps coming, I'll meet him where I am.

The Kayan kept coming—earrings swaying, curved leopard teeth on a necklace swaying, too.

Harry had played rugby in school, and he was a good batter in cricket. Now he gripped the stave like a cricket bat. The

Kayan didn't slow down as he drew nearer, but kept up the same bobbing pace. Closing on Harry, he raised both the parang and the spear-tipped blowgun.

Harry waited, a sudden calm in his mind as if he were watching this happen from afar. He swung the stave in a quick, looping arc, stepping aside as he did so to avoid the Kayan's parang. The stick caught the Kayan in his midsection, doubling him over, and Harry's second swing came down on the crown of his feathered head, crumpling him.

Now Harry turned and ran, wondering if he could find the Iban. Zigzagging among the hardwood trees, he was feeling that they had gone on without him when a beckoning hand appeared around a frond. Then he saw Tambong's face.

She was smiling.

He followed the smiling face into a deep thicket, his gaze fitfully catching a brown leg or arm. Then he was with them, all three suddenly beyond this forest, facing a sandstone cliff.

"Akai!" Bayang exclaimed in dismay as he stared up at the wall, whose reddish cast had the demonic look of iron skin.

With the intuition born of excitement and danger, Harry knew they were trapped.

He followed the Iban alongside the cliff, while from the jungle they had just left came the whooping of gibbons that were not gibbons. A dart nicked the cliff just ahead of Harry and fell to the ground. Glancing at the jungle, he saw nothing.

"Akai!" Bayang yelled again, this time triumphantly, for he'd discovered a fissure in the cliff. They raced through the rocky passageway and beyond the cliff into another stand of forest. Harry breathed a sigh of relief, only to see, when they had reached the cover of jungle, yet another dart, this one pinging against Bayang's uplifted parang.

Two Kayan appeared in the undergrowth, their own parangs raised. Harry experienced a frightening instant in which he stared at a high-bridged nose and plucked eyebrows and smelled the pungent odor of sweat and loamy earth before bringing his stave down against a dark cheek, splitting it open like fruit.

From the corner of his eye he saw Bayang scuffling with the other Kayan, both falling, and Bayang's parang going up and flashing down bloodily through the leopard war coat of his adversary. To Harry's surprise the girl rushed over and caught Bayang by the arm, dragging him off the fallen warrior. Bayang seemed furious at the girl and flung her away. For a moment he hovered above the Kayan, whose wide-eyed stare signified death. For a moment longer, Bayang held his parang as if ready to cut off the Kayan head. The moment passed. He chose the option of escape and led the way on.

Harry followed the Iban into the jungle, hearing the thud of feet, the heavy pulse of breathing. Finally Bayang halted, one foot raised as if he were made of stone. The girl crouched behind him, and Harry tried not to breathe loudly. Reaching over his shoulder to the quiver, getting a dart and putting it into the blowgun, Bayang eased forward with such a snakelike motion that his bones seemed unhinged. With infinite patience he raised the weapon slowly to his lips, but before getting it there, he uttered a short call, a hooting sound such as an owl made. There was movement ahead in the bush. Bayang put lips to mouthpiece and blew one powerful breath into the blowgun. There was a cry beyond the foliage, a human cry. Bayang waved his companions in another direction, and they plunged deeper into the forest.

How long did they trot forward without stopping? Harry had always been athletic, but the jungle humbled him. Stretched out exhausted on the ground, he stared at the uppermost branches of a rain tree where a giant sloth was gripping a limb.

The sluggish animal looked like a great bundle of laundry tied up in a brown sheet. How peaceful the sloth seemed up there, claws inching stolidly along as if the air they pushed against retained the viscosity of mud. Harry watched a long time, entranced, half dreaming, then turned his face on the humid earth so he could study Bayang. The Iban warrior seemed dejected in spite of their escape from the Kayan.

Harry had been out here long enough to understand. Having killed his adversary, the Iban should have had his reward: a head. A realization that would have disgusted Harry before traveling with the Iban did not disgust him now. He accepted Bayang's feeling of disappointment as reasonable.

When the young Iban warrior saw that Harry was regarding him, he smiled, and when Harry sat up, he saw Tambong smiling, too.

Bayang pointed to the stave lying beside Harry and smiled more broadly.

So the second time out, Harry thought, I was not a coward. Nothing in his life compared to his sense of contentment at that moment.

Getting to her feet, Tambong took a section of bamboo from her belt and removed the leaf she had corked it with. She offered the bamboo to Harry, who upended it and let the honey inside slide down into his mouth. The profoundly sweet taste invigorated him instantly.

When he gave the honey back, Tambong took some for herself.

Harry nearly asked if they had escaped from the Kayan, but thought better of it. Such a question would be foolish. There was no way of telling. Each moment of their lives was separate from the next, and therefore precious, and therefore unique. Perhaps this was always true of the jungle; might well be the deepest secret of the jungle: the now of it was everything, and time in a sequence meant nothing. Harry felt proud of living so completely on the edge of time. He lay back and within seconds fell asleep.

Sure of him sleeping, Bayang said to the girl, "The Kayan took the body away. There's no chance of going back and finding it."

"I know. Forgive me," Duck Foot said with downcast eyes.

"No, I won't forgive you. That head was mine to take."

"If you stayed there long enough to take it," Duck Foot told him boldly, "your head would now be theirs."

Bayang knew that was probably true, so he said no more. In fact, he never again mentioned the Kayan head.

"Harry is more than we knew," Bayang noted after a long silence.

"His mother helped him. She's protecting us all," Duck Foot declared. "Sleep awhile. I'll stay awake and watch."

So Bayang curled up and like the other boy fell instantly asleep. Duck Foot watched over them both while the sun arced from overhead to a position halfway to the ground. In the slow procession of time, Duck Foot let herself think quietly, thoroughly. She knew certain things. She knew that the obat of the aahkit was very powerful, for it had led them away from the Kayan war party. Not a single dart had hit them. And the obat had given the white boy a semblance of Iban courage, enabling him to fight like a true warrior. But she also knew that without the right dreams, Bayang would never find the Big Fish, and those right dreams must come from the Goddess of Sleep. Bayang awakened first. Anxiously she awaited word.

"I think I dreamed about hunting," he admitted glumly, "but I can't remember."

"It'll get better now," she reassured him, though without reassuring herself. "The Goddess of Sleep is pleased with us."

.

But two days later, still meandering in a southwesterly direction through the rain forest, Bayang had received nothing from his dreams. They were as barren as a keranga—land unable to support a rice crop.

They stopped for the day in a small clearing surrounded by tall casuarina trees with pale fissured bark and frizzy crowns of leaves. They ate a macaque monkey, brought down by one of Bayang's darts. It was of the lion-tailed variety, black, with a huge mane around its face. While the poison worked, it had thrashed on the ground, squealing like a human baby. Harry winced.

Bayang looked drawn, perhaps even sick, and certainly glum, as he sat by the fire, holding a half-eaten leg of the roasted macaque. All day, he told Duck Foot, birds had crossed their path from right to left instead of left to right—a bad sign.

When Duck Foot offered him a papaya, he refused. Today, when he'd gone alone down to a riverbank for a drink, he'd seen a banded kingfisher perching on a limb over the water. Its large crested head had moved slightly in a search for fish below. It gave a sudden cry, a prolonged rattling sound. Then it flew away. When a kingfisher gave its call, then flew away without first taking a fish, it was a bad sign.

Duck Foot did not add to his discomfort by telling him of her own dream last night. It had been of rocks rolling down a cliff and a box turtle pulling its head inside its shell, slowly, again and again and again. This was a dream of warning. Rocks falling meant danger. The turtle pulling its head inside meant they did not know what they were doing.

What concerned her more than the dream, however—after all, hers was merely the dream of a woman—was Bayang's state of mind. She had come to believe in his mastery of a warrior's skills and his great soul, but she also knew his weakness: he became discouraged. He could fight, he could make decisions, he could lead others, but his own dark thoughts sometimes settled round him like a thick mist through which he could see nothing.

They could not wander forever through the jungle, waiting for the Goddess of Sleep to release them from torment and let Bayang locate his destiny. They must make things happen. Duck Foot resolved to act, even at the risk of Bayang's becoming angry.

Turning to Harry, she asked him to tell them about his mother. Where was she now? What pleased her? What made her angry? How did she come to him? To emphasize her request, Duck Foot got up, went over to Bayang, and lifted the locket up from his neck, snapped it open, and displayed the red-haired woman inside.

What happened then made no one happy.

On his feet, excited, Harry began talking rapidly in English. He spoke of his childhood, of his school, of his parents and how each died, of England, of the Windsor tradition of service to the Crown, of his own resolve to follow in the footsteps of his ancestors, of his mother's beauty and gentleness and strength, of his own despair when she died, of his loneliness, of his need for the locket, which was all he had left of her.

When abruptly he ended the long rambling monologue, Harry looked from one Iban to the other and gloomily sat down.

They had understood nothing.

But Duck Foot turned to Bayang and said in rapid Iban, so that Harry couldn't piece out some of the words, "It's what I expected: he won't give up the obat. He will die first. His mother holds on to him. What we must do is separate them." Then she explained that a visiting dayung had told their own dayung what to do if a powerful spirit attached itself to a human. You put the spirit back into the earth, where it lost its memory of this affection. When you dug it up again, the spirit had forgotten everything. It was new and ready to find another loyalty. But there was danger. For two days the spirit must remain in the ground; during that time fires might break out, cobras come into longhouses, rhinos stampede through rice padis, floods overturn boats. It was a time of struggle and possibly of death.

For a response to her warning, Bayang removed the locket from around his neck. "Here is the aahkit."

"If you want it done."

"I do. Bury the aahkit. And if there's danger, can it be worse than what we face now—day after day of wandering? Bury it. Let's try for dreams."

With her anak parang, the girl dug into the soft earth and soon made a hole a foot deep. She placed the locket inside and covered it up.

"Wait!" yelled Harry, getting to his feet. "What's this? That's my locket you put in there!"

Instantly Bayang was on his feet, too, the spearpoint of his blowgun only inches away from the white boy's heart.

"That's my locket," Harry declared again, looking at the small mound of earth. "You can't just bury it like that!"

Duck Foot, squatting beside it, patted the mound. "Bayang," she said with a wan smile. "Life." Then she lifted her hand from the mound, as if surrendering the locket inside. "Death." She held up two fingers. "Two nights."

As night descended, the three sat in the small clearing, watching one another grow dim, indistinct, then fade into nothing but the faintest dark outline against the darkness. Then each assumed a position of sleep, but clearly none slept.

After a while, Harry sat up and edged over to the mound, now visible in a few glowing rays of moonlight.

Bayang sat up, too.

Harry didn't move.

They faced each other with the mound between them. Both stared at it a long time, and from where she lay on her side, Duck Foot fearfully studied one boy, then the other.

The moon had passed beyond the clearing when Harry, with a sigh, lay down at last, and then so did Bayang, and the three troubled wayfarers went to sleep.

·13·

For two days they rarely left the clearing except to find food: mostly fruit and wild vegetables. Duck Foot brought in two handfuls of snails, and after a short hunt Bayang returned with a flying squirrel. Harry never left at all, but sat cross-legged most of the day, staring at the mound beneath which lay the portrait of his mother.

His captors seemed nervous; any sound in the forest startled them. When he asked if they expected another raid by the Kayan, they stared blandly at him as if such an attack would be the least of their worries. Surely their pervasive fear had to do with the ritual of burying his mother's portrait. It strengthened Harry to know that he didn't share their superstitions and fears. He merely sat there near the buried locket, protecting his property from further harm, while both Iban glanced fearfully around, eating distractedly, remaining silent most of the time as if lost in thought or awaiting catastrophe.

A renewal of self-confidence, augmented by peace and quiet, prompted Harry to think again of escape. He couldn't have explained exactly why, but he knew that his captors were embarked on an adventure quite beyond his ability or his inclination to share. Moreover, it was linked to the portrait of his mother in some illogical and savage way. Their minds were filled with beliefs and images that might drive them to do things horrifying, barbaric, vicious. In spite of that, Harry admired them for their persistence and their courage—indeed courage, for whatever they hoped to accomplish by burying the locket, they were doing it at some profound personal risk. He had to admit that the Iban were as strong and brave as anyone he had known, including his parents and his uncle and the tracker Abik. Not that he liked them. They had kidnapped him and taken from him his most prized possession; though he and Bayang walked the same jungle path, they were as far apart as if they lived on different planets.

Harry found himself protesting his difference, emphasizing to himself his knowledge of the world beyond the jungle and their ignorance of it, until the odd but very real possibility occurred to him that he was afraid of succumbing to their way of life. Out here they knew what they were doing, and so he was tempted to view them as wiser than himself. It was true. He willed himself to cling to his British tradition. He struggled to remind himself that he was a Windsor. He faced a very real threat these Iban represented: if he followed their ways, he left behind the whole of European civilization. Was their life really so tempting? He admitted that it really was. In truth, aside from moments of extreme danger, he was living the best part of his life right here in the Bornean jungle, where time was always now and the vast ocean of greenery washed over him like an endless dream.

A spear traveled differently from a dart because each possessed a different spirit. When you uprooted a plant, you released its spirit, so you should always apologize for doing it. When you killed an animal, its spirit fled into the air like smoke. Everything that was, was spirit. Spirit let itself be known through the call of birds and through omens; a wise man listened and looked. A dream was the meeting place between spirit and spirit; it was where you found the truth.

When he wasn't anticipating a terrible event, brought on by the buried aahkit and the struggle of a goddess to separate herself from a human, Bayang was thinking such thoughts. Never had he felt so close to the spirit world or so fearful of it. He understood now many things about Iban life that he had taken for granted before. For example, after the rice harvest, when the dayung summoned back home any lost spirits wandering across the stumbled padis, the living protected the dead. Bayang appreciated that now: how they merged together like water in water, so that the ancestors lived fully in the present and the living had the dead at their shoulders. He had a sense of time moving in a circle the way a man lost in the jungle finds himself returning to the same tree, the same bush, the same river.

As time passed, he felt less threatened by the possibility of death or injury occurring to Duck Foot or himself. The buried aahkit would do them no harm. Yet he also felt that something was about to happen.

If only they could rid themselves of the white boy, Bayang felt sure that things would go better. Harry was nothing but trouble. Harry was always watching them, studying them the way a hunter studies the spoor of a stalked animal. He felt Harry's eyes fixed on the aahkit. Did Harry know they were trying to separate him from his mother? What would he do if he did find out? Attack! Surely. Desperate for the return of his goddess-mother, Harry would use his last strength to get her back. So they must not tell him if he didn't know.

The second night, both Iban stayed fully awake, staring at

the small mound of earth, waiting for something to happen. His own sleep fitful, Harry often awakened with a start, then leaned forward to make sure that the mound was still there, untouched, before sliding again into sleep.

Toward morning, suddenly, Bayang fell asleep, too.

He paddled alone in a dugout canoe down a river. The canoe grew longer and longer until it was as long as their Iban longhouse, and then it filled up with people familiar to him: his mother and father, his brothers and sisters, his friends, the warriors, the dayung, and everyone else. Searching frantically, he located Duck Foot, who sat alone in the bow of the canoe, watching for submerged logs. He paddled far until all along the bank appeared the white men with whom Harry had traveled and then there stood Harry himself, smiling and waving as the canoe passed by. The sun rose high on Bayang's left arm, and through its brilliant rays he saw a bird flying. It was a Brahminy kite, the chief omen bird. It was the great god Lang Sengalang Burong in the form of a bird, leading the way downriver, guiding Bayang along until he could see, when the channel narrowed to a width scarcely wider than the canoe, a white man seated on a throne that glittered on the surface of the water. Rising, the white man bent forward in a bow of respect, while Bayang left the canoe, walked across the water, and took his place beside the white man on the throne. The great chair of power then turned and headed farther downriver. Like a kingfisher perched on a limb in a search for fish, Bayang leaned over the throne's side, searching . . .

Duck Foot was looking down anxiously at him when he awoke.

"Something happened," she whispered tensely. "I saw it in your face while you slept."

So he told her the dream, after which Duck Foot silently dug up the locket.

"They are separated," she told Bayang. "The goddess is now loyal to you."

"The dream was very great."

Duck Foot nodded in agreement, glancing over at the white boy, who, after a difficult night, had fallen into a deep sleep at dawn.

"The dream was very great," Bayang repeated, "but I'm not sure of the meaning."

"The goddess has told you where to go and what to do," Duck Foot declared. The canoe growing as long as the long-house was a sign that the Iban people somehow shared his destiny. She explained that traveling with the sun on his left arm meant he was heading for the coast. He was going to the great city of the white men. That's why the white men stood on the bank: they were welcoming him to Kuching. And because Harry was among them, smiling and waving, the white boy must be returned to Kuching and his brothers. There was no doubt of the meaning. It was made clear because the great god of the omen birds, Sengalang Burong, led the way downstream. This was the truest guide possible. The white man on the throne was the Rajah himself, called Rajah Buk, who would share power with a great Iban warrior. In the last part of the dream, when Bayang peered at the water like a kingfisher, he was searching for the Big Fish.

Yes, it was a great dream, Duck Foot declared. The Goddess of Sleep had told him he must go to Kuching and take Harry with him. If he did so, he'd find the Big Fish and the true answer to his life.

When Harry awakened, he knew something momentous had occurred, not only because the locket had been removed from the ground and replaced around Bayang's neck, but also because both Iban had changed. They no longer seemed fearful; in fact, they seemed intensely happy and excited, and with the disappearance of their lethargy came such a renewal of energy that Harry was hard put to keep up with them as they moved swiftly through the jungle. At last they were going somewhere specific. This was no longer a dreamy meandering through the rain forest but a purposeful trek that reminded him of his uncle's expeditionary force moving inland from the coast, bent on getting information. The Iban said little to each other or to Harry, but headed out as if a huge magnet were drawing them implacably onward in a direction north by northwest. That surprised Harry, for it meant that the Iban were heading toward the coast. But would they sustain this heading? Perhaps before reaching there, they'd turn back inland and make for their own longhouse or for the trackless eternal forest again. He asked during a stop for rest.

"Your longhouse now?" he said to Tambong.

"No," said Bayang.

"Then where?" he asked Tambong.

"Out there," Bayang replied, waving vaguely ahead. Only the Iban warrior spoke to him anymore. The girl never did, not even when Harry addressed her directly. In the last day she had waited for Bayang to answer every question. Tambong was obviously deferring to the warrior in Bayang, and a measure of this deference was that he alone might speak to the captive.

What had happened, Harry wondered. When he fell asleep, they had been two frightened natives. When he awakened, the young warrior had assumed the arrogant mien of a chief and the girl had taken on the role of a subservient woman, and both of them seemed absolutely determined to go somewhere, to do something.

In this purposeful mood the Iban traveled alongside a small river that would inevitably meet a larger one and ultimately a river large enough to be known by them. Harry no longer needed to be told such things.

On the first day they came upon a large river turtle, three feet across, with a leathery green neck and blocky head. Working together—Bayang with his blowgun and Harry with his stave—they were able to turn the animal over on its back. It had huge webbed claws that contracted against the air. The webbing reminded Harry of Tambong's foot, but that didn't give him any sympathy for the turtle when Bayang slashed two, three, four times at the head. Harry drove his pointed stave between the belly plates, eased it into the soft flesh of the heart area. When the two boys had killed it, Tambong slit it open with her anak parang, and all three worked to pull its guts out. The surface of the river was frothy with fish eager to get at the entrails thrown back into the water. The girl cut up the choicest sections of meat, while Harry helped Bayang salt it down for taking along and cooking later. Harry smelled the pungent odors of blood and fat and bowels while his hands became slimy with grease, slick mossy scales, blood both gouty and thin.

That evening, when Tambong mixed the blood with sago flour, as she had done with the wild pig, and boiled it in the pot, Harry waited as impatiently as Bayang for a taste. And after he ate, Harry licked the rust-colored mess from his fingers with such gusto that both Iban laughed.

So efficient were the Iban on the trek that it took them only two days to reach their goal: a briskly flowing broad-backed river. Leaning on the blowgun, Bayang stuck his chin out, smiled, and turned to his captive. "Rajang," he declared.

So they had reached the renowned Rajang, a river that snaked through mile after mile of jungle to the sea, one of the great riverways of Borneo.

Tambong hardly glanced at the impressive river before starting a search along the bank for soft-fibered leaves. Having collected some, she chewed them into a paste. This was to stanch a flow of blood from cuts Harry had just incurred. Before reaching the water, they'd passed a stand of elephant

126

grass whose serrated edges had slashed Harry half a dozen times without his realizing it.

Watching her smear the leafy salve on his bleeding skin, Harry asked suddenly, "Are we going down the Rajang?"

Tambong acted as if she hadn't heard him. She kept rubbing the paste into his arms and legs.

During the application of this medicine, Bayang vanished without a word—simply disappeared. Accustomed to decisions being made without his knowledge, Harry sat down beside the girl and waited. He kept busy by brushing away sand flies that hovered in roiling clouds around his head. Tambong sat in a way that hid the webbed toes of her left foot—left leg crossed under her. So accustomed was Harry to her affliction that it startled him to realize the girl felt ashamed. Her sensitivity confirmed what he'd been thinking for the last day: he didn't understand the Iban at all. Were they really savages? After all, what made them so? Fighting? Warring? His own father had died fighting in a war. What they ate? Europeans ate snails and brains, too. How they dressed? He used to laugh at the tall wigs and silk breeches worn by men in the eighteenth century—and the full-bottomed wigs still worn in British courts. Did the Iban's ignorance of things Western make them savages? But how many people in the West were ignorant of things Iban? Harry wondered how on earth he had ever looked upon these people as childish. Where had he got the idea? Surely the Resident had encouraged him to think so. And in truth a boastful arrogance had helped him confront the rigors of the jungle, at least in the beginning. Now he no longer needed to get his strength from a pose of superiority. It occurred to Harry that he had learned a great deal about surviving out here. He didn't need to flatter himself, not anymore. He could accept the Iban for what they were, and himself for what he was, and that meant none of them had anything to defend.

But when he glanced at Tambong, ready to announce this discovery, the girl seemed unaware of his presence. The Iban were not interested in letting him into their secret world. Harry turned away and sat up ramrod-straight, as he'd been taught in school. He was getting into the habit of slouching the way Americans were said to do. Remember, you have centuries of British tradition to uphold, Harry told himself. But the warning seemed mechanical, as if he were reciting a passage in Latin by rote.

Abruptly the girl got to her feet, shaded her eyes, and stared upriver. At the far bend a canoe appeared.

Bayang was paddling.

Somehow he had commandeered a canoe or stolen it. Tambong said nothing about his acquisition of a boat, and certainly Harry wasn't going to ask. Out here you did what you had to do. Harry would not have been surprised to see dried blood on Bayang's parang the next time it was drawn. In fact, he was mildly surprised to see none when Bayang unsheathed it later to cut off some turtle meat for cooking. So the Iban warrior must have stolen the canoe from a village or longhouse.

Tidak apa, Harry told himself in Malay. It didn't matter. Out here what mattered was surviving or getting where you wanted to go. Surviving and getting somewhere were the same thing to the Iban. He could fathom that from the grim determination in their faces. Whatever the Iban warrior and the girl were doing meant life and death to them. And their goal had something to do with his mother's portrait.

That bothered him deeply, because sooner or later he must take the locket from them.

· 14 ·

So their meandering trek through jungle turned into a purposeful boat ride down a river that flowed nearly four hundred miles from its jungle headwaters to its wide delta on the South China Sea. In places it narrowed and grew so shallow that boulders loomed out of it like the glistening backs of sporting whales. Once through an undergrowth of assam paya—palm trees hardy enough to live in tides of shifting mud and tangles of ribbon-like parasitic roots—Harry had a glimpse of wild water buffalo, lying spread-eagled in swamp water, with only their faces and horns showing. Sitting in mid-canoe, he saw olive-colored macaque monkeys scrambling through trees along the riverbank, scolding the boat and its occupants. And when he finally took his turn paddling (insisted on it!), Harry watched cuckoos with brilliant plumage racketing in mossy ironwoods and Malay parrots peering from liana vines that corkscrewed around towering rain trees. He saw mouse deer sipping elegantly from the river and gray-faced buzzard eagles hovering above the forest canopy while ground mists hovered below, as thick as cream, among oleanders and ferns and orchids in the rattan groves that the canoe passed.

Sometimes the river widened into a slow flat fluidity of brown water, at which times Duck Foot sat in the bow and kept a sharp lookout for submerged logs that might drive a gaping hole into the boat's side. There were long hours during which nothing seemed to happen, but for Harry they were magical. The jungle foliage that he idly gazed at was sometimes so thick that it seemed to have a film spread across its leaves, a wide expanse of intricate webbing that gave this greenery the look of something solid without differentiation within itself, something as democratic as water; if it moved, it moved as a complete mass, not tree by tree, root by root, leaf by leaf, but as a single living body, pulsing with one breath.

For these moments of suspended time Harry was grateful. It was an interlude outside of his own history that allowed him to step away from his troubles and hopes and where, quite beyond them, he could be a witness to nature and its own ways and see it going on with no interest in him, wholly indifferent to whether Harry Windsor lived or died, but in spite of such indifference just as alive as he was. Linked by this timeless journey to the Iban, Harry felt closer to them than ever before, so close that he wondered if he could leave them.

But that was before signs of human life began appearing on the river: driftwood with nails in it, a pearly oil slick from an engine exhaust, an opened sardine tin floating like a tiny boat, a piece of red sarong, a rubber sandal chewed ragged by river fish, then an orderly pile of immense teak logs stacked along the shore, and the rotten hulk of an abandoned dugout. Each symbol of man's encroachment on the river seemed to affect the Iban, who grew silent, morose, nervous, as if already they were challenged by forces unknown and inimical to them.

On the river and its bank there was more and more debris: pieces of atap roofing, some logs bound together with rattan, an old tire that might have been lying on the rocks for years,

Harry thought. Such debris now signaled security as if he were looking at signs of home.

Then a canoe with an outboard motor passed them, going upriver. A turbaned Malay who handled the tiller gave the Iban a dark frown. Not an hour later came a dugout carrying at least a dozen Malay passengers in Western trousers and white shirts with soft collars. Clutching bundles, they were headed for riverside marketplaces called bazaars or logging camps far inland or villages called kampongs, which were backwater settlements composed of atap-roofed shacks. Harry knew he would soon have a choice either to stay with the Iban or escape from them by asking loggers or villagers for help. Civilization was on its way, and in proportion to its increasing appearance he expected to feel more detached from the Iban.

Unless they about-faced and returned to the jungle, he'd have his freedom without their consent. But from their determined expressions, Harry felt certain that neither of the Iban would run for safety. Set on this course, they'd never stop before reaching their goal, whatever that was.

At a curve in the river they came suddenly upon a logging camp. There was a rusting crane and a godown filled with logs thirty feet long, six feet around, and a cluster of dormitory buildings with sloping zinc roofs, and a rickety dock to which was tied a flat-bottomed barge and an old scow hung around with tire fenders like a huge string of ugly beads. Loggers gave the canoe an idle glance, no more, and went about their business. It was the first civilization that Harry had seen in weeks, and the sight nearly brought from him a wild Huzzah! so excited and happy was he, even though the camp itself seemed dilapidated and filthy, with its cabins of peeling gray boards and muddy walkways. He stared at one curtainless window that had an outside shelf, and on that precarious narrow board sat a pot of red flowers, just like ones he might have seen from a train window coming into a sooty industrial town, say, Leeds or Liverpool.

On the outskirts of the camp there was a vegetable garden with staked pepper plants and cabbages. Gripping a hoe and wearing a conical sun hat was a Chinese gardener, stripped to the waist, grinning at the passing canoe. Harry might call out Help! and then dive into the water and swim ashore. Behind the garden, built on a cleared hill, stood a church on stilts with a big cross above its square wooden frame. There were Christians here who would help him. But Harry sat there motionless while Bayang paddled them on. He felt as though he couldn't move. Why? Couldn't he leave without the locket? Or was he curious about the Iban and their reason for going downriver? Or did he simply want to stay with them?

Civilization was already changing the Iban—he could see it in the wary look of their eyes, in the taut lines around their mouths, in the hesitant, perhaps even confused way they stared at the logging camp, the crane, the lumber barge. Perhaps he might reason with them or threaten them with punishment once they reached a proper town. But punishment for what? Looking back at his capture, Harry saw it for what it was: their way, somehow, of protecting themselves. Maybe he should promise to help them in whatever enterprise was taking them so far from their own people. But would they believe him? What held Harry back was his uncertainty about their belief and trust in him.

That night when they stopped and made camp along the riverbank, Harry resolved to confront his captors and find out where they stood.

They had eaten smoked mouse deer, guavas, and jackfruit, and in the firelight sat back from the riverbank to watch the fireflies add their own darting luster to the luminous moon glowing down on the broad iron back of the Rajang.

Bayang had removed both knives and scabbards from his belt, along with the blowgun and quiver. He was unarmed, in a state of unreadiness reserved for nighttime after a meal, although one knife was always in reach.

Duck Foot found herself glancing often at Harry, who seemed unusually watchful and alert. She nearly warned Bayang, but without having more reason for it than their captive's restlessness she'd succeed only in irritating him. Iban warriors made a great show of contempt for a woman's fears. Even so, she kept watching the white boy as he shifted position, played with a blade of grass, and sank deeper into whatever thoughts were plaguing him like sand flies.

Then at last Harry spoke. His words in English and broken Iban, accompanied by gestures, took a long time to understand, but finally it was clear: he wanted the obat of the red-haired woman and he wanted it now, and if Bayang didn't give it to him, he would take it. It was an open challenge to a fight.

Bayang nodded quietly and stood up. So did Harry. They faced each other in the firelight, each waiting for the other to do something.

Duck Foot squatted nearby; her anak parang was still in her belt, but to use it under any circumstances would violate Iban law. A woman must never interfere with combat between men. There was nobody in the world who meant more to her than Bayang; she had acknowledged that to herself long ago, near the outset of this journey. But she couldn't protect him from an enemy's challenge. If she interfered and Bayang died, his seven souls would never cross the bridge into the Land of the Dead but would howl like mad dogs on the muddy bank forever.

So Duck Foot squatted, waited, and ignored the knife in her belt. Perhaps nothing would happen, she thought. They might circle like two young rhinos, snort awhile, paw the ground, then trot away in opposite directions. And sure enough, both boys stood as motionless as stone, their features deepened by firelight into the masks of two angry but fearful beasts.

Then Harry put out his hand, palm up, flat. "Give it," he said in Iban. To make sure he was understood, the white boy touched his throat where the locket had once hung. Then he pointed at the chain around Bayang's neck. "Please," he said in Iban, "please give it."

"No."

Harry took a step forward, hand still out, his voice ominously calm as if, Duck Foot thought, he had spirits around him, ready at his call to help. She felt a chill even as he asked again, "Give it, please," while balling both fists and coming forward.

Bayang didn't bother to say no, but stood with both feet planted wide. This enabled him to take Harry's first blow, which came almost instantly, without falling down. But Harry's other hand caught Bayang on the chin, hurling him near the fire. He was bent over on one knee, shaking his head to clear it, with the white boy standing over him.

It was then that Duck Foot understood fully how much bigger Harry was, his muscles more prominent, his whole body far more powerful. All this time she had taken Bayang's jungle skills for sheer physical strength, but in truth the awkward Englishman, ignorant of the forest, had the real brute power. And when Bayang staggered to his feet, Harry proved it again by smashing him with a big white fist. He didn't fight like an Iban, with kicks and holds, but with his hands wielded like clubs. The first few blows had hurt Bayang so much that he couldn't recover and mount a kicking attack. Twice, feebly, he kicked out, but the white boy stepped aside and hammered him three, four, five times. The last blow lifted Bayang up and slammed him to the ground.

"Give it to me," Harry commanded, his fists making tight, fierce little circles in the air over the fallen Iban. "Please, Bayang, give it up."

"No."

Harry waited until the Iban again got to his feet. Asking him once more to give it up and receiving no answer, Harry struck him so hard that blood flew. The next blow knocked the young Iban warrior down.

Duck Foot noticed a change in Harry's expression. He no longer seemed angry or even powerful; on his face was a look of . . . she didn't know of what, but it was not that of an enemy bent on finishing off his opponent. He was saying things in English, his voice almost soft and gentle, as if he was pleading with Bayang, while the Iban slowly, silently, but implacably worked to get himself back on his feet.

Harry still talked as if pleading. And he was. She realized that. Harry didn't want to hit Bayang anymore; he even backed off a few steps when the Iban lurched at him, blinded by blood in his eyes. Bayang kicked out, but spun and fell, breathing heavily. Then, while Harry pleaded with him to stop, he struggled to his feet and shuffled toward another closed fist.

Reluctantly, withholding real power, Harry tapped him on the cheek, and Bayang went down like a felled tree.

Harry knelt beside him and touched his shoulder. He was whispering things in English. Then in broken Iban he declared, "Do not give me it. Keep it, you. Yes. Keep it." He tried to help Bayang into a sitting position. When he'd succeeded—Bayang but half-conscious—Harry said it again, "Yes, keep it. Keep it, keep it."

Why had he changed? Duck Foot wondered. Then it occurred to her that the Goddess of Sleep, the red-haired woman who controlled the obat, had told him what to do. The goddess didn't want him to have the obat back. She wanted him to give it to someone who needed it more. So it was true that the goddess now favored Bayang.

Duck Foot realized she must have been smiling with relief, because she met Harry's astonished eyes and heard him say, "Smile? Why? You smile?" while taking out a torn kerchief from his pocket. In English he mumbled, "What sort of people are they, when I beat the hell out of her friend and she smiles about it?" He began to wipe blood from Bayang's face.

For two days they remained in this clearing beside the riverbank, with the canoe pulled ashore and hidden within palm fronds in the undergrowth. For two days Duck Foot administered to Bayang's cuts by making poultices of weeds and leaves. Little was said by anyone. Harry spent much of the time brooding, his back against a tree trunk, his eyes fixed on a trail of elephant ants trundling eternally across the leaf-strewn ground. Bayang was no less thoughtful, his gaze steady on the muscular flow of the great Rajang. Once, however, he said to Duck Foot as she worked on his cuts with a plaster of chewed weeds, "He told me to keep the obat. Why?"

"The goddess ordered him."

"He's very strong."

Duck Foot shrugged dismissively. "He fights in a strange way. All with his hands."

"What does he think of me?"

"He thinks you're brave."

"You think so?" Bayang asked nervously.

"He knows you are. If you were not, the goddess would take the obat from you. But she wants you to have it." Duck Foot added thoughtfully, "He is now wai."

Bayang stared at the girl. How could a white man ever be a true friend of the Iban? But perhaps she was right, because the spirits had given Duck Foot vast powers of knowledge. Without thinking more, he got painfully to his feet and walked over to Harry and squatted beside him. Pointing first to Harry, then to himself, he declared, "Wai."

Harry knew the word. His eyes grew wide and his mouth opened in surprise. Then in Iban he said, "Yes. You, me, friend." In English he added rapidly, "You need the locket more than I do. I never saw anyone take such a beating. You're braver than all my classmates ever were. My God, yes. It's my privilege to be your friend. And that's not all. Whatever it is you want to do, I'm going to help you do it. Because you want it so much. Because I wish I wanted something so much, and so I've got to help you get whatever it is, and that's what my mother would want—the lady of the portrait would want. She'd say, 'Harry, for godsake, lend them a hand and don't ever ask for the locket again. They need it a lot more than you do. So help them, Harry. No more thinking about it, just get on with it and lend a hand. There's a good boy.' " He caught himself talking to himself—and in a sense his mother talking to him— aware that the Iban understood not one word of what he'd been babbling. So after pointing to himself and then to Bayang, he merely said in Iban, "I . . . you . . . friends . . ." He balled a fist and waved it at Bayang's chest and at his own and then circled it in the air.

Duck Foot came over to squat beside Bayang. Both Iban looked at each other.

"Does he mean to help us?" Bayang asked her.

Duck Foot looked with keen appraisal at the white boy's solemn face. "Yes. He means to help us find the Big Fish. It's what his mother wants from him. Harry will help us. He knows what he must do."

They turned and grinned at Harry, whose broad pale face lost its severity and broke into a smile, so that all three were smiling and reaching out and touching each other's shoulders and faces with fingertips, as if discovering one another for the first time. Bayang then rummaged through his knapsack until he found the knife he'd taken from Harry. Handing it over, he said, "Friend."

Harry studied the knife as if seeing it for the first time. Taken from him and returned, it had become a symbol of trust and friendship.

"Big Fish," Bayang said happily.

"Big Fish," Duck Foot repeated.

Bayang put the palms of his hands together and wriggled them like a fish going through water. Then he spread both arms to encompass the entire jungle. "Big Fish!" he exclaimed. Crouching, he looked from side to side as if searching in the undergrowth.

Harry understood. "Yes, I'll help you find the Big Fish," he said in English. "We'll do it together. It's a promise!" he swore happily. "Yes, we'll do it! We shall!" His voice booming across the rain forest startled a bevy of starlings so much that they flew from their perch in a tree, their wings beating like a thunderclap, their black shapes rising in the bright sky like a storm cloud.

·15·

N ow the trio set out as a single will, committed to a search for the Big Fish, although for Harry the Big Fish was still an Iban mystery and this journey to the coast had the added dimension of returning him to his own people.

The Iban stared in wonder at kilong traps along the river-bank: spiral-shaped fences made of closely set poles driven into the river mud to a depth of two feet, ten yards in diameter; they watched fish enter this maze on the ebb tide, work around to the center of the spiral; a sliding gate fell and imprisoned the fish so they could be taken out with a hand net. Bayang had feathered the paddle of their canoe for a long time near one such kilong, studying the contraption.

Harry wondered if the Iban warrior was thinking of taking back the idea of a kilong to his longhouse. Somehow this journey was a heroic search for something, with Bayang regarding his people's destiny as his own. Harry didn't take it for arrogance. The strong ambition in his friend was what he expected of himself, too. He was learning to think of them as linked by the desire to excel rather than separated by the customs of England and Borneo.

During the days now they encountered river traffic: dugouts, wooden-hulled launches, shallow-draft cargo boats, and high-pooped Chinese junks, all of them headed upstream between formidable walls of mangrove. The swamps of uniform green were unbroken for many hours save here and there by the flickering white shapes of feeding egrets.

Sometimes people on the shore waved idly at the canoe, sometimes not. It didn't matter to Harry. What did matter? Merely the long, slow hours of paddling down the Rajang, the evening fires on the shore, the deep sleep and mist-heavy mornings, and the taste of wild fruit before setting out on the river again. If it were not for his worry about the fate of Uncle Julian and the expedition, Harry would have paddled on forever, spending his life magically on the Rajang, together with his friends.

But as the miles drifted by, bringing him closer to the capital of Sarawak, he felt an end to the contentment of such travel and a beginning to the fear of getting bad news in Kuching about his uncle.

This fear prompted in him a reluctance to get there. When finally he saw the big paddle steamer tied up to a jetty, he nearly signaled for Bayang to continue on past this rather large riverside bazaar. As they glided near the jetty, with a sigh of decision Harry motioned for the Iban to pull in. Without hesitation Bayang did, as if, unlike Harry, he was prepared for an encounter with townspeople, though his eyes seemed hooded in wariness, his lips pursed tensely.

The paddle steamer, a substantial four hundred tons of hardwood and iron, was called the *Cantik*—the "Beautiful" in Malay—though there was little about the overworked old scow that could be called beautiful. Its gray paint peeling, its lines chafed, its metal parts rusting, it plied the Rajang from

Kuching to villages upriver, carrying salt and tools to the interior and hauling rattan, raw rubber, and deck cargo downriver and along the coast to the capital. It was captained by a weather-beaten old Malay who called himself Leman. His mate was his twenty-year-old son Bandong, an extremely fat young man who was never seen on deck when he was not munching something and who never, never worked. The remainder of the crew were a long lean Chinese engineer and two undernourished coolies who handled lines and swabbed decks and endured the shouted abuse in Malay of Captain Leman and his son Bandong.

When Harry Windsor appeared on board, Leman took one astonished look at his white skin and greeted him like a long-lost nephew. To Harry's instant question about the fate of the expedition, the old sailor shrugged apologetically and shook his head. He'd heard something about the expedition and its ambush by natives, but couldn't say for sure what had happened. Some of the men had returned, he thought, but some had been killed, to the best of his recollection. As to the expedition's leader, well, he wasn't certain. That's all he could remember, he confessed with a grin and another shrug.

Harry was dumbfounded by such indifference, but then he was not yet acquainted with the peculiarities of Captain Leman or of his son. It would take him, however, only a day aboard the *Cantik* to fully realize their interest in him. Perhaps they expected a fine reward for returning him to Kuching—as if they had rescued him from marauding headhunters!

Had they not valued him so highly, they might have refused to let the Dayak natives on board, but Harry's absolute insistence on treating the Iban with courtesy won their reluctant compliance. They allowed the Iban on board the steamer, then, with still more reluctance, let the tribals share a tiny cabin with Harry—all three sleeping on the hardwood deck, though Captain Leman offered him the mate's well-appointed cabin if he occupied it alone.

While Chinese merchants were loading the boat for its return trip downriver, Leman drew Harry away from his Iban companions and regaled him with tales of vicious headhunters who smiled one moment and slit your throat the next. Harry's failure to react to such news prompted Leman to further vilify the tribes. He leaned toward Harry—his head scarcely reaching the tall boy's shoulders—and in good English announced hoarsely, "The Dayak measure wealth in terms of wine jars and gongs and bags of salt. When they get angry, they fight, and when they fight it's to the death, so to get angry for a Dayak means to kill someone. Or if they don't kill because of anger, they kill because of what they dreamed the night before. That's right." He grinned, revealing a line of broken teeth. "These people depend on dreams. Dreams tell them what to do and how to live. If a dream tells them kill, they kill. And when dreams don't control them, spirits do. They see demons everywhere. They are"—against his skull, matted with luxuriant black hair, he made a screwing motion—"crazy. They catch souls in the air like other people catch balls. They're not really human. Me, Mohammed Leman, I am Muslim. I believe in Allah. But these Dayak, they believe in devils inside the bodies of frogs and tree trunks and mostly inside of birds. A Dayak is always deceitful, untrustworthy, savage. The Dayak, all of them, whether Iban or Kayan or Penan or anything else, they're all crazy, mad, undependable, vicious. It must have been Allah's merciful will that they didn't murder you out there in the jungle. Allah be praised!" But though he raised his hands in ecstatic blessing, from the corner of his eye Leman could see that he hadn't roused the white boy at all. On the contrary, the boy yawned as if bored.

Having failed to get anywhere on the subject of Dayak

treachery, the sly captain turned to the faults of the Chinese. He seemed to hate them more than the Iban because they dominated trade along the river. There were the hot-tempered Hakka, the cunning Foochow, the numerous Hokkien and Cantonese and the Hylam, the Henghua, the Teochiew, all of them doing brisk business everywhere in everything and in the process cheating both Malay and Dayak innocents out of their rightful possessions.

What Harry learned about the Chinese was their fearsome energy as he strolled with his gawking Iban companions through the bazaar. Sugar, cloth, beans, salt fish, cooking oil, and soy sauce were sold there, along with gamelan gongs and tinned goods and earthen tubes of preserved duck eggs and Singapore wine. Every merchant burned smudge coils in his shop to keep away swarms of mosquitoes. There was a terrific din of dialects everywhere, as the merchants argued furiously with customers and one another. There were sewing machines for sale (the Iban stared at them in wonder) and gramophones and cups of Ovaltine.

Harry noticed that in the tumult of the bazaar Duck Foot tried to conceal her limp. She bit her lip in the effort to walk evenly. At ease in the jungle, confident and proud, here she was timid, uncertain, embarrassed. And when they halted to sip tea at a canopy-covered stand, instead of squatting in traditional Iban fashion, she sat cross-legged on the ground, hiding her left foot from view, gulping the cupful all at once. Harry glared defensively at passersby who stared at the two upcountry natives.

When the *Cantik* got under way again, its deck was overloaded with penned pigs, caged ducks and chickens, stacks of alligator skins, bundles of rattan and raw rubber, baskets of live crabs and unripened wild fruit, and bamboo sections filled with hot peppers. As they steamed along, Leman insisted on

Harry's company in the tiny wheelhouse. Harry had the feeling that the captain was keeping watch over a prize possession. Leman, smoking a huge cheroot, kept one gnarled hand on the wheel and the other on Harry's arm, gripping it to emphasize a point he was making. As they navigated down the Rajang, he insisted that without his help there was no chance of a young white man and two Iban reaching Kuching.

"Pirates go up and down the Rajang as they please," he claimed grimly. They left the *Cantik* alone because they knew Leman. He had once been a companion in their looting and plundering, he was ashamed to say, all along the Bornean coastline, until religion—praise Allah!—had convinced him to give up his sinning ways. "My old mates would never set foot on this boat, never. They know the wrath I'm capable of," he boasted, patting his holstered pistol. "You are safe." He squeezed Harry's arm. "Traveling with natives in a canoe, you'd have been easy prey. River pirates would kidnap and hold you for ransom, and once they had the money . . ." Taking his hand from Harry's arm, he made a slashing motion against his throat. "Believe me. The authorities think the Rajang's as safe as a pond, but what does government know? We coastal-water captains take chances. We deserve a bigger share of profits from cargo." And he went on, becoming lost in a rambling diatribe about the discrepancy between his measly pay and his peace-keeping efforts on this river. Without him the Rajang would be a place of thievery and massacre; he alone, steaming up and down the river, enabled people to live decent lives. Tears of self-pity and righteous indignation filled his eyes. "Praise Allah you reached the *Cantik*. If pirates didn't get you, those two thieving savages would have finished you before you got within a day of Kuching."

Coming into the wheelhouse with a runny mass of durian fruit in his hand, the fat son Bandong ate noisily and belched.

From piglike eyes he watched the river and nodded in agreement with his father's outcry against injustice. Putting down the cheroot, Leman picked up a soapbox filled with fresh raw garlic, the cloves of which he proceeded to peel deftly and pop into his mouth like peanuts. The stench of Leman's breath, along with the grim oratory, drove Harry out of the wheelhouse and back to his cabin, where he found the Iban, both sitting on the deck staring at the peeling bulkhead.

He sat beside them and waited until, after a long silence, Bayang spoke. "Iron Fish." He slapped the deck. "Does it go to Big Fish?"

Harry threw up his hands in helpless reply to a question he didn't fully understand. "Iron Fish to Kuching." He felt with dismay that they were depending on him. Becoming wai with the Iban was very serious. Friendship brought responsibility. "Iron Fish to Kuching," he repeated. Seeing disappointment in their faces, Harry added with forced enthusiasm as he pointed to them and to himself, "Then all go to Big Fish!"

He watched their lips tighten. Yet their eyes remained wide and bright, which meant to Harry that they still trusted him and hoped.

At sunset Captain Leman brought the *Cantik* close to the riverbank and anchored. Bandong was eating and belching loudly amidships. To avoid more of the captain's lectures in the wheelhouse, Harry stood at the stern, looking down at the swirling water. He had left the Iban in the cabin, both sitting cross-legged, staring at a bulkhead.

Suddenly he noticed a long, narrow dugout approaching the starboard strakes. Hardly any time elapsed between his seeing the boat and a dozen men leaping upward to scramble over the gunwale. There was enough sunlight left for him to make out turbans, baggy trousers, and rifles held overhead.

River pirates. Harry had only an instant to think of this before they reached him. Their Malay was too quick for him to understand a word, but he understood the intent of their shouted commands. He thrust his hands upward, and immediately other hands raced over him with the swiftness of scampering mice, tapping his pockets and removing what was there: a piece of salt fish wrapped in a leaf, some wadded money. Soon Bandong appeared, hands also over his head, with two men prodding him forward at a waddle. Next came the captain, tight-lipped and submissive, between two Malays. Shoving their captives together, the pirates whispered among themselves as if deciding what to do.

"Talk to them," Harry urged, turning to Leman. "They know you, don't they?"

"Ah, I'm afraid not. They aren't known to me. Not these men."

Harry glanced at the little captain, whose gun was missing from the holster, and realized that his claim to former piracy had been an empty boast. "What now?" Harry asked in a low voice.

"Ah, I'm afraid we're in trouble. Have you any money?"

"What little I had they took."

"Ah, we'll need a lot more. Your uncle—how much would he pay in ransom?"

"I don't know. I don't even know if he's alive."

"But the other Englishmen in authority—how much would they pay?"

"I don't know."

The pirates, all short and swarthy men, were still arguing. Now and then one of them glanced over at the captives, then said something.

"Are they going to murder us?" Harry asked in growing fear.

"Ah, I'm afraid they're unhappy. Let me talk to them." Leman spoke rapidly in Malay. This brought him into a brisk discussion with the pirates, who waved their hands and pointed their guns at Harry.

"They want you for ransom," Leman told him. "These are very bad men. They'll want plenty. Will your Englishmen come through?" When a pirate said something more, Leman turned and entered into what Harry could only guess were negotiations of some kind.

A few of the pirates were probing around the deck, lifting canvas, poking at bales, discovering what might be worth taking. And then one of them cried out.

Squinting at the Malay who had yelled, Harry saw a dart sticking in the man's arm. A rivulet of blood snaked between his encircling fingers as he yipped from the pain like a dog. Another yell. A pirate staggered and bent over, gripping his side. A third pirate shot his rifle into the air, then leaped over the gunwale into the dugout. In a fit of frustration a fourth pirate fired wildly in Harry's direction, the bullet grazing Bandong's fat cheek. And yet another yell. This time one of them toppled to the deck, the eight-inch shaft of a dart halfway into his throat. The remaining pirates, some of them shouting frantically, went over the side—a few leaping into the river, from which they were hauled into the dugout. And as quickly as they had appeared, paddles flashing in a final slant of sunlight, they vanished around a bend in the river.

It was then that Bayang, blowgun in hand, scrambled off the raised bow, with Duck Foot limping behind him.

The Chinese engineer and crew peeked from nooks and crannies, then rose to their feet, grinning as if they had contributed to victory. Scowling at them, Captain Leman turned to his son and examined the superficial cheek wound. Then he muttered, "Those devils weren't known to me. I thought I'd sailed with the worst, but this was a new lot of them.

This never would have happened had they been old-timers."
Harry regarded him a moment, then frowned. "We were lucky to have this thieving, untrustworthy Dayak aboard."

The captain seemed too lost in his own musings to notice the sarcasm. Bending over the pirate hit in the throat, Leman shook his head. "He's murdered. Your Dayak is a fierce one. They must have thought he was a dozen brutes!" The captain sighed as if disappointed. "You picked yourself a good brute, though. He saved you a lot of trouble and your people a lot of money."

Walking over to the Iban warrior, Harry clapped him firmly but gently on the shoulder. "Good friend," he exclaimed in Iban.

Next day the *Cantik* reached the sea and headed down the coast lined with mangrove swamp. Four days later they steamed into the harbor of Kuching, bringing with them an oil slick and a swooping band of sea gulls and in their wake a playful school of freshwater sharks.

Shading his eyes from the glare of high noon, Harry anxiously scanned the waterfront crowd that awaited the *Cantik*'s arrival. There was no familiar face. Looking at the bridge, he saw Captain Leman waving him up. Climbing the rickety ladder to the wheelhouse, Harry took the outstretched binoculars from the little captain, who urged him to look. "Your uncle! Over there? He may be there!"

While Harry stared through the twin glass circles at a crowd farther down the shore, Captain Leman said, "God is great whatever happens. Perhaps your uncle died quickly. They say the Kayan prefer quick kills, not like the Ukit and the Kadayan. Not like the terrible Iban brutes. Praise be to Allah! Your uncle was in the hands of quick-killing Kayan!"

Harry felt his hands trembling so much he couldn't hold the binoculars steady, but then into his vision came a tall figure in white, with flaring blond sideburns and a pith helmet and a cane held across his broad chest.

"Uncle Julian!" Harry cried out.

Taking a huge puff on his cheroot, Captain Leman nodded with satisfaction. "So my prayers were answered. Just as I thought! Your uncle lives. Praise be to Allah!" And seconds later he added, even while maneuvering the paddle steamer alongside the crowded dock, "Please tell the Senior Enforcement Officer, your illustrious uncle, of my significant part in your escape from the jungle. Never forget. Without the *Cantik* you'd not have seen Kuching again."

His son Bandong, a man of few words, chewed thoughtfully on a piece of smoked mouse-deer meat and touched his bandaged cheek before adding his own sage observation. "Yes, Father is right. You owe us your life."

·16·

For many days Julian Windsor, Senior Enforcement Officer of Sarawak Protectorate, had been meeting every boat that entered Kuching harbor, hoping against hope for news of his nephew from anyone coming out of the interior. He never expected Harry to be on board one of these river boats—that would be a miracle.

Yet today a miracle occurred: squinting through the noon-day haze at a weather-beaten old paddle steamer, he saw on the bridge, face obscured only partially by binoculars, a broad-shouldered red-haired European boy; within seconds he realized it was, without doubt, his lost nephew Harry, about whom he had worried endlessly since the Kayan attack.

Within minutes they were embracing on the dock to the astonishment of the Chinese and Malay witnesses, who believed that Britons lacked emotion. They were laughing and shouting at each other, asking questions there wasn't yet time to answer, especially because Captain Leman had reached them almost as quickly as they had reached each other.

"Good sir, honorable sir!" The captain plucked at the officer's sleeve. "We took good care of your nephew, sir!" Leman boasted, while a gawking crowd gathered around. "Think nothing of his passage downriver. I throw that in free."

"We were attacked by river pirates," Harry said.

"What?" Officer Windsor turned to the captain.

"Ah, well." The captain shrugged it off. "They gave us only a bit of trouble."

"My friend here—" Harry pointed to Bayang, who stood with blowgun and parang at the fringe of the crowd.

"What?" Uncle Julian stared a moment at the Iban warrior, then turned back to the captain. "How did this happen? Attacked by river pirates? The Rajang's been quiet for months!"

"We anchored offshore one night," Harry volunteered when the captain said nothing.

Looking the little man up and down, Officer Windsor asked impatiently, "Why on earth would you do that? Anyone on the river knows you must always tie up at a dock. You're asking for trouble otherwise."

"I thought it was safe," Captain Leman said. "I was in a great hurry to return your nephew."

"Have your ship's papers at my office tomorrow," the officer demanded severely.

"But, sir, is there no reward?"

"Reward? There's no doubt in my mind you arranged for the boarding. They knew beforehand." He turned to Harry. "Did you stop at a market or town along the way? You did? Well, then, this scoundrel must have sent word to have these men board at a designated place. Without the help of your . . . friend"—he glanced through the crowd at the Iban—"they'd be asking a huge ransom by now. And your savior here"—he glared at Captain Leman—"would have been waiting for his own cut."

"But, sir—" began Leman.

Wheeling around furiously, Officer Windsor led his nephew out of the crowd and stopped to gather in the two Iban. As they walked up the wharf, he whispered to Harry, "We won't prove anything tomorrow. At least we'll frighten him enough so he won't try it again. Indeed, your Iban friend saved you. How did you ever . . . We'll need time to sort everything out."

Uncle Julian was too overjoyed to regard the two Iban accompanying his nephew with more than passing curiosity. On their return to his cottage in the hills just outside Kuching, he merely nodded in casual assent when Harry asked that his friends be quartered in the house. And he waited suspensefully while Harry, like a good host, saw to it that the Iban each had a room and something to eat, though the Hakka cook seemed unhappy with the prospect of preparing food for Dayak natives.

On the veranda, over iced tea and biscuits, Julian at last sat down with his nephew for a long talk. He found it impossible to get anything out of Harry, however, before first telling the story of the expedition and what had transpired after the Kayan attack.

Julian stared tensely into the sultry afternoon air. They had lost two men, two others were badly wounded, and three more sustained minor wounds.

"Lost two," Harry murmured. He recalled, as he had many times during the last few weeks, the sight of the man ahead of him going down with a dart in his back. "Was one of them the Iban Rentap?"

"He died that night. The dart had been poisoned. Another Iban died the next day. Henderson was slashed in the face with a parang—cut half through his jaw. He's still in the hospital."

"And Abik?"

"I really think he saved us. He lashed out with absolute ferocity, taking on three Kayan with his parang. They yelled out he was a demon." Uncle Julian guffawed. "I say, they bloody well *meant* it. Demon! They might have kept fighting had they thought Abik was merely human. They took him for an evil spirit, and so they ran. We killed five of them—Abik two by himself. Then he disappeared."

Harry nodded. "Of course."

Julian Windsor narrowed his eyes. "Whatever do you mean—*of course?*"

"I'll wager one of the dead Kayan disappeared, too."

"That's right, one did."

"It's what Bayang would have done, too. Abik dragged off a man he'd killed and removed the head. He couldn't stay with the expedition then, could he. Abik must have gone back to his longhouse with the head and held a great celebration."

Julian smiled wryly. "You've learned a good deal, nephew, since I last saw you. We understand that's exactly what Abik did do. He returned to his longhouse—and held a feast. I suspect after a while we'll see him again here."

"What will you do when he comes back?" Harry asked anxiously.

"Why, nothing. He's a splendid tracker. I won't mention the head. If he admits taking it, of course, I'll have to jail him. It's the law."

"He won't admit it," Harry said with relief. "The Iban know how to play the game."

Studying him a moment, his uncle said quietly, "And perhaps so do you." He continued with his story. "After that single attack, we never saw the Kayan again. They went about their business, no doubt going after weaker prey. We limped back to Miri and caught a coastal ship for Kuching, and here we are." He stared hard at his nephew, as if reliving the torment of these past weeks. "We thought you were taken by the Kayan for a slave. Or they killed you and left the body out there somewhere. So now, lad, tell me about you."

•

After Harry had related his story, Uncle Julian sat in a long, thoughtful silence before commenting. "I noticed the Iban is wearing your locket. Knowing how you feel about it, I'm sure you didn't give it voluntarily. He must have taken it. What I'm not sure of is why, after your fight with him, you didn't demand back what was yours."

"He needs the locket more than I do."

Julian's eyebrows raised in surprise. "The thing you cherish most?"

When Harry gave no further explanation, Julian let the subject drop. What was important, from Julian's point of view, was his nephew's honest admission of panic during the Kayan ambush and then his courage during the second Kayan attack when he traveled with the Iban. Harry had made up for it, proved capable under fire when given another chance, so his decision to let the Iban boy keep the locket was something Julian decided not to judge. He had faith in his nephew because his nephew had earned it.

"Why did the Iban come downriver with you, Harry? I don't understand that."

"They're in search of something. It has to do with my locket and with what they call the Big Fish. It's not clear if it's really a fish they're after. I think it all comes from a dream."

"Ah, one of the deep dreams of the Iban." Julian shook his head disapprovingly. "There's no people like them for believing in dreams. That makes the Iban difficult. You can't deal with them on the basis of reality; you must take into account their dreams." He sighed. "I hope, Harry, you don't involve yourself in their odd problems."

"I'm already involved."

"Oh, really?" Uncle Julian's tone became sarcastic. "You're going to search for this big fish of theirs that lives in a dream? Where will you look? How big is this big fish? How will you recognize it, assuming you find it? Assuming you can separate a dream fish from a real fish? Must you dream of it, too, in order to find it?" Julian threw up his hands irritably. "Leave Iban things to the Iban. They're the only people in the world who can deal with themselves."

In a low, calm, even voice, Harry told his uncle, "Sir, I will help them however I can."

"I'd like to know how."

"For one thing, I'd ask a favor of you."

Julian eyed him suspiciously. "What kind of favor?"

"Will you send for Abik at his longhouse? He's Iban, he'll know how to talk to Bayang. He can be my interpreter."

Julian stroked his jaw awhile as if uncertain how to treat such a request. Finally, with a sigh, he said, "Ordinarily the answer would be no. Let Abik come back when he's ready. But I sense in you a stubbornness that's—well . . . you've come through with flying colors. Jolly well done, Harry. Yes, I'll send for Abik."

Abik did not live far upriver, so word was sent by Officer Windsor on the next cargo boat going that way. Meanwhile, Harry took his Iban friends to the waterfront markets, to the manicured parks and public buildings, to the Sarawak museum with its stuffed animals and Dayak artifacts, at which they stared in disbelief, as if unwilling to believe that anything of their people might leave the jungle and reappear under glass. He persuaded Uncle Julian to take them to lunch in a Chinese restaurant, where they ate with their hands and spit out food they didn't like. Harry strolled with them along the wharves at sunset when the sun was a perfect circle of burning coal that cast a path of molten crimson across the Sarawak River. When a river barge broke through the surface and left swells and ridges in its wake, the solid path of late sunlight scattered into the look of tiny red flowers flung across the water. The far riverbank was hazy from the smoke of cooking fires. Palm fronds clutched the final sunlight like fingers until sky and forest merged all together and assumed the uniform blue depths of deep water. Harry wished they had in common another language so they could speak of such a beautiful moment. Harry wanted to tell the Iban how much he liked Borneo—*loved* Borneo was truer. But all he managed to do was grin and point at the sunset and mumble in Iban, "Good," to which both Tambong and Bayang replied with a polite and simple "Good."

On the third morning after their arrival in Kuching, Harry got out of bed and walked past the two bedrooms where the Iban slept. Both doors were open, so he looked in and found the rooms empty. Running out into the garden, he glanced wildly around, fearful they had simply left and gone home to their longhouse. They mustn't go yet! he thought. They mustn't go until they find their Big Fish.

To his relief, Harry discovered them wrapped in bedsheets, lying side by side asleep under a frangipani tree.

He got from them that a demon of some kind lived in Duck Foot's room, so they'd left the place to its evil occupant and come out here to sleep in safety. Puzzled, Harry urged them to go back inside with him and investigate. The Iban squatted solemnly in the room and cocked their heads as if listening intently.

Harry listened, too.

Then he heard it: a faint *tick tick tick* from the metal-framed clock on a dresser. A servant must have put it there last night, as he would have done for the use of any guests. But these were guests who told time by sun and shadow. Picking the clock up, Harry held it first to Duck Foot's ear, then to Bayang's, and said in English, "Clock . . . clock . . . no antu buyo. Only clock ticking. See? Tick, tick, tick."

The Iban nodded politely, but refused to sleep inside the house again. Harry had a Malay gardener make room for them in the tool shed, and that was where they remained during their stay with the Senior Enforcement Officer of Sarawak.

Uncle Julian was not amused by the story or tolerant of the Iban behavior. He used it to drive home a lesson. "Harry, it must surely be clear how different your world is from theirs," he said as they sat in his book-lined study. "Why not reward them for helping you and send them home?" After a pause, he added with a frown, "Though I must say there are strong legal grounds for detaining them as kidnappers. I've taken no action out of deference to your feeling for them. But I see unhappiness and confusion in their faces, Harry. Some Iban prefer civilization, but clearly these two don't."

Instead of responding to his uncle, Harry asked if any word about Abik had come downriver.

"No, none has."

"I think he'll clear up a lot of things."

"Very well," Uncle Julian said testily, "have it your way. Englishmen come out here with all sorts of pretty ideals, and soon enough the heat and hardship and difficulty with the natives change them or they go home broken and sometimes mad."

"I don't have any fancy ideals, Uncle Julian. I just want my friends to find their Big Fish."

Next day the Iban tracker Abik appeared at the cottage door, asking for the young tuan. He began talking as if nothing had happened to either of them in recent weeks. Having been put at ease, Harry explained his desire to help two Iban friends in search of something they called the Big Fish. Motioning the tracker to walk with him in the garden, Harry couldn't hold back his curiosity but whispered in Abik's ear, "Did you take a head?"

The leathery tracker halted to emphasize his displeasure. He frowned severely. "Not me, tuan. Never. Taking heads is against English adat."

"But not against Iban adat," Harry said with a smile. "You can tell me. Did you have a feast?"

"Not me," Abik declared forcibly. "English adat mean more than heads."

When Harry chuckled at the lie, Abik smiled broadly. "Be good, tuan. Do your friends teach you to make jokes like an Iban? Take me to them."

That evening Harry reported to his uncle at dinner (Bayang and Duck Foot had gone with the tracker to eat with a family of urbanized Iban at the edge of town). "It's what I hoped. Abik gained their respect immediately and they told him everything. Bayang had a dream. In it he was swallowed by a big fish, and inside its body he was able to look at the world through the eyes of the fish. Bayang saw everything, the entire world— green below, blue above. Then the fish spit him out, telling him that if ever he swam again inside its belly, he'd know the secrets of the world and become a great man for his people. The fish told him to watch the duck flying when he searched in the waking world for a return to its belly. The duck flying is Tambong. In the longhouse they call her Duck Foot because of the webs between her toes. So she has had to go with him, and if he doesn't find the Big Fish again, his dream will rot inside him and destroy his soul. That's where my locket comes in. They see in my mother's portrait a goddess who controls dreaming. Through dreams she'll tell them where to look for the Big Fish. You see? It's logical, sir. And a matter of life and death."

Uncle Julian smiled tightly. "Whatever happened in the jungle has made a powerful impression on you, Harry. I think you're drawing me into this odd affair, too. Against my better judgment, I might add. So there you are. I'll do what I can to help."

"I'm grateful, sir." Without hesitation—suggesting he'd thought of his next request long before dinner—Harry said, "There's a way you can help. Bayang must depend on the duck flying, but Tambong can't fly the way she is. Her crippled left foot is like a broken wing. I was wondering. You once said Dr. Tomlinson is a good doctor, wasted out here, when he could have had a big London practice. I wonder."

"Yes, lad, go on."

"Could Dr. Tomlinson take a look at her foot? Maybe something can be done."

"I see. You mean, so the duck can fly?"

"And search for the Big Fish."

Uncle Julian shook his head slowly, a gesture of puzzlement and disapproval. "The jungle has changed the complete Windsor I knew into someone part Iban. Clarity has always been the hallmark of a Windsor. Now you're swayed by dreams. Some people would call that weakness."

"Like the Resident? He never lived in the jungle with the Iban. Mother and Father would understand. I think they'd feel I'd gone beneath the surface of things. And they'd like my friends."

After a moment's thought, the officer nodded in agreement. "I'll talk to Tomlinson."

· 17 ·

No one could talk Duck Foot into seeing the white dayung—not Harry, not Abik, not Dr. Tomlinson himself. Duck Foot hid behind some rakes in the tool shed and refused to come out when called, begged, pleaded with, when voices were raised in Iban and English, supplicating and cajoling: "Please allow the good doctor to have a quick look, please, even at a distance, say, from across the garden, would you please, just hold up your foot and let him study it from afar, because please, he won't hurt you, just one look, please!" Bayang, who squatted beside her in the dim wooden enclosure, wore his parang and was prepared to use it in her defense. He shared her fear of white magic.

Officer Windsor speculated wryly that they might remain in the tool shed indefinitely—after all, the Iban were known for stubbornness and pride. And indeed, a whole day passed without their leaving the shed.

During this time Bayang joined Duck Foot in ignoring everyone: the Malay servants, a British orderly, Officer Windsor, Harry, and even Abik, their fellow Iban. Bayang squatted beside the girl and waited for something to happen. That was what they would have done in the forest. But there they'd have so many signs to read and act upon: the precise and varied way a branch tilted or a bird sang or a wind came up. He didn't trust the town of Kuching to give them messages of equal importance. What Bayang did was think hard about the Big Fish. There was nothing else to do, so he thought and thought until it occurred to him that they were ignoring the Goddess of Sleep. Removing the obat of the red-haired woman from around his neck, he put it around Duck Foot's, startling her.

"Wear this aahkit and dream," he said.

His generosity of spirit encouraged her to accept the bold idea of the goddess speaking to her instead of to him.

That night Duck Foot touched the aahkit when she went to sleep. She dreamed, and next morning told him her dream. A white egret flew over the longhouse and circled it many times, while Duck Foot waited for the padi bird to fly away or come down. At last the bird flew down and told her she must fly, too. Flap your wings hard, the bird explained. So Duck Foot flapped her arms hard, but she couldn't fly. Climb on my back, the egret commanded, and we'll go together, but when we get high enough, you must fly on your own. So she climbed on the white bird's back and they flew into the sky. When they were far above the ground, the bird told her to fly on her own, and this time, when Duck Foot flapped her arms, she flew. She flew alongside the egret until she approached the sun, where her seven spirits melted and fused into one soul. This single spirit descended until it reached the longhouse, where it entered Bayang's heart. Then he flew upward and became a twinkling star.

"The obat of the red-haired woman has favored you with a strong dream," Bayang declared happily.

"I must fly or you'll never find the Big Fish again." Limping briskly, Duck Foot emerged from the tool shed with Bayang following her. Below Harry's bedroom window, she called out, "I go to the dayung!"

Later that day Dr. Tomlinson would inform Officer Windsor and his nephew that the examination of the girl's foot was very encouraging. Webbing between the toes could be surgically removed without trouble. Once healed, her toes would be as strong as ever. No longer needing to compensate for the webbing, she'd walk normally.

She nearly got up from the elevated board on which they'd placed her and almost ran away when one of the white women approached with a dart in hand. White people didn't use blowguns, Duck Foot thought, but jabbed you when you were down. It was all she could do to remain quiet and accept the dart and what might be its poison. But the dream sent by the Goddess of Sleep must be obeyed. She felt only a tiny prick and it was over. An Iban dart, she thought proudly, would have gone the length of a finger into her arm. This one merely nicked. She lay back and let the magic do its work. Sure enough, she got sleepy and was only half-aware of being moved on the board somewhere. She gazed woozily at white walls and white men in white before another white woman came alongside and shoved something over her face, and she could fight no longer against sleep.

Next thing she knew, her eyes opened wide and she was looking at another white room. Her left foot hurt with a throbbing pain. When she peered down at it, it was not there. For a terrifying moment she wondered if they had cut off her foot, but they had only covered it in white cloth. The pain from each toe traveled upward along her leg the way liana vines climb up a tree trunk. She lay in this white room for two days. People came in, smiling, and gave her food and round little white things to swallow, like bitter berries. They took the cloth off her foot, bathed the hurting toes, smeared something like chewed leaves on them, and told her, "Don't worry," in poor Iban, "Don't worry, don't worry." The pain didn't matter, because for the first time in her life she saw each toe on her left foot move separately from the others. The duck-foot webbing was gone.

When Bayang was brought in to see her, he carried a small gift of food from the bazaar: a "sausage" of roasted glutinous rice and a cake called lompor sorga—"heavenly mud."

The girl demonstrated for him how she could wiggle her bandaged toes. "The Goddess of Sleep spoke in a true way. She said fly, and so I will. The white dayung's magic is good."

"You can be tattooed now," Bayang observed with a smile.

"I can do more than that. Watch the duck flying, the Big Fish told you. I will fly."

"Yes, but how?"

"We must wait and see how."

"But fly where, Tambong, and how?"

"We must wait and see. Please, not Tambong. Call me Duck Foot."

"You won't be—"

"I will always be Duck Foot. I used to think if only the webs were gone and I walked like any girl, I'd be different. I'd be Tambong and only Tambong. But I'm not different. I'm still Duck Foot. Only one thing has really changed. Now I can fly. Do you believe me?"

"I believe you. But how? Where?"

Pursing her lips firmly, Duck Foot said, "We must wait and see."

Days lengthened into weeks. The Iban waited and saw nothing but daily evidence of Duck Foot's recovery. With the aid of a cane she shuffled around the garden, then struggled without the cane. A pronounced limp faded and finally vanished.

But she wasn't happy, a fact observed by Officer Windsor.

"Here we've done everything possible for the girl, but you'd think she was worse off than before the operation."

"It's because she's ashamed of not flying," Harry explained. When Uncle Julian rolled his eyes in exasperation, Harry added, "You see, without her help Bayang can't find the Big Fish. According to his dream, he must watch the duck fly."

"Are they waiting for a dream? Is that what you're telling me?"

"Or for something to happen. For a sign."

"All I see is them walking or sitting in the garden. And you too," Uncle Julian added disapprovingly. "It's not my idea of searching for something."

"But it's theirs. In the jungle they'd have many signs to look for."

"Very well, then. Why don't they return upriver and look for signs in the jungle they know?"

"Nothing's told them to do that. So they wait."

"They've been here a long time, Harry. I don't mind feeding them, but frankly, I think they're making you lazy."

Harry said nothing, because he didn't know how to explain that being with the Iban could never make him lazy. True, they did little during the day. Duck Foot showed him how to weave baskets with liana vines and Bayang helped him to become a fairly good shot with the blowgun—they practiced on a target painted on the tool shed. But they also introduced him to the silent communion of their special world. Often they sat together for an hour or two without a word being spoken, hardly moving, yet they communicated in a way that would be inexplicable to Uncle Julian. In unison, as if linked by invisible wire, their heads turned to pick up the faint trill of a distant bird.

They studied the clouds as with one pair of eyes. They sniffed the drifting smoke of a market fire, inhaling simultaneously. At such times Harry felt they were a single consciousness.

And yet Uncle Julian was right: because of her failure to fly, Duck Foot was becoming increasingly grim and unhappy. Bayang squatted beside her with the stoic look of an Iban warrior, but Harry knew him well enough to feel his frustration. He had journeyed all this way in search of the Big Fish, but not a single dream or sign had told him where to go next or how to search further.

Nevertheless, Harry would have continued to wait with the Iban in this interminably patient manner if Uncle Julian hadn't interfered.

"The three of you should get out of this garden," the officer told Harry one afternoon as they sat under a banyan tree. "You ought to see the Vickers Vimy that came in yesterday, Harry. It was originally a twin-engined bomber, but after the war they removed its guns and refitted the bomb bays with extra fuel tanks. Its range is now seven hundred miles. Didn't you tell me you liked planes?"

"I once saw a Handley Page O/400 parked in a field near London. It was a twin-engined bomber, too. The Vimy has a range of seven hundred miles?" Harry whistled.

"It's on a promotional tour for a company going into the mail carrier and cargo business. Came over from Singapore. Why not gather up your friends and we'll go see it? Near the tobacco godown south of town. They're using the field there for an airport. Rollins is the pilot, an old friend of mine from the war. He'll let us look around." Officer Windsor tugged at his sideburns. "It's bloody time you got up and went somewhere, Harry. You might even cheer up your friends."

That last remark brought the red-haired boy to his feet. "Yes, sir," he said. "Maybe it's worth a try."

·

When they arrived at the field, Officer Windsor led them around a large shed to confront the Vickers Vimy. To the Iban it looked like an immense insect or a bird from a nightmare. Four men came from the shed, all white men (two staring from what seemed to be frog eyes). They walked forward smiling, shook Officer Windsor's hand and then Harry's. Then they stared curiously at the girl in turban and sarong and the boy with distended earlobes, a two-foot parang stuck in his rattan belt, and bluish-black tattoos on his dark chest.

Harry walked over to him, touched his arm lightly, and pointed at the mysterious object. "Vimy," he said.

For Bayang, this Vimy had nothing to do with his world. It didn't even look like something that should exist. Bayang had no use for the thing, consequently felt no interest in it. He squatted down and waited politely, while the white men, including Harry, studied it in detail as if it were a captured leopard.

The Vickers Vimy had two sets of wings, the larger set spanning sixty-seven feet. The Rolls-Royce Eagle twelve-cylinder water-cooled engines revved up to 360 horsepower and cruised at 118 miles an hour. The fuselage, made of spruce, was covered with white fabric, and within the cockpit, which was big enough for the seated pilot and navigator and for three or four people standing behind them, the dials and gauges of flight control were displayed across the instrument panel: airspeed indicator, altimeter, rate-of-climb indicator, bank indicator, revolution counters, fuel-flow indicators, compass, and radio transmitter.

None of this was known to Bayang, who would have been indifferent to such knowledge anyway. He must simply show Iban courtesy and wait until it was time to leave.

But then Harry, smiling in anticipation, came over and squatted beside him. Through gestures, Bayang realized that Harry wanted him to go closer to the thing. Harry made a swooping motion into the air with his flat hand.

Like a bird flying.

Duck Foot, who had been standing behind them a few paces, came forward quickly. She repeated Harry's gesture and turned to look at the thing.

Harry nodded. "Yes. We go," he said, pointing at her, Bayang, and himself. "We can go inside," he said in English. "My uncle's arranged it. We're going for a ride!"

Bayang never moved but remained squatting, idly tracing his finger along the ground. Abik had told him that white men did silly things at times. What were they going to do with the big dead insect? He glanced in surprise at Duck Foot, whose eyes had a sudden light in them.

"We'll go with them," she told him. "It will go there." She looked upward.

"It means nothing to us."

"It means I will fly. Just as the Big Fish said." Without waiting for his response, the girl turned and headed briskly toward the waiting group of men.

Harry motioned at the Iban warrior. "Come, Bayang. Please, come."

He would not have gone for Harry, but Bayang understood that the Iban girl had recognized a sign. Perhaps it was the one they had been waiting for. He rose and followed where Duck Foot led, joining the others at the open door of the thing.

He found himself trapped in a small enclosure containing things that clicked and blinked. Duck Foot stood next to him, lips trembling, eyes shining. He looked ahead through what he didn't know was a glass window at a wooden-bladed propeller.

Two of the white men, those with frog eyes, sat down in the seats. Everyone else stood behind them while they pulled at the clicking and blinking things and turned them and pushed them until a terrible noise issued forth, like a rainstorm filled with thunder, so that they could hear nothing else and the big sticks began to whirl around so quickly that Bayang could see them only as blurs.

The noise grew louder and then, to Bayang's dismay, they began to move. He nearly lost his balance as the huge thing rattled and shook and swayed from side to side. Imitating Duck Foot, he grabbed on to something jutting from a wall and held on for dear life as a queer sensation came over him, unlike anything he had ever felt before, and when he opened his eyes—for he'd shut them tightly—Bayang no longer saw the closely cropped field or, beyond it, a mangrove swamp. He saw only sky that stretched on and on like a depthless blue sea.

Harry touched his shoulder and pointed from the window vigorously. Bayang had to take a step closer to the cockpit window; once there he peered down at what appeared to be a flat lawn of greenery. Leaning forward until his forehead touched the glass—its unyielding surface making him jump back for a moment—Bayang could see that the lawn was actually composed of countless green trees. A forest was passing with such quickness that he hardly saw one tree before seeing another. Looking up, he located nothing there at all but a sea of blue, no hills or tall trees as he would have seen while looking up in a rain forest. Nothing obscured an unruffled surface as blue and calm as a pool in deepest jungle.

Green below, blue above—as he had seen in the great dream.

Then the truth struck him so violently that he gave a sharp cry and the others in the cockpit turned to regard him curiously.

Where was he?

Inside the Big Fish!

This was the Big Fish! Duck Foot had led him to it. Turning, he shouted at her, "The Big Fish!"

She smiled faintly but didn't seem to understand. "Flying," she told him. "As the Big Fish said."

"The Big Fish!"

She had brought him to the thing but didn't yet know it for what it truly was. He knew because the dream told him. Once again he was inside the belly of the Big Fish, looking out from its eyes at the world.

Exuberantly, Bayang regarded the passing jungle below, a part of it approaching and a part receding at a speed easily matching the speed of things in dreams. As the Big Fish swam through the sky, it allowed him to see for the first time the true vastness of the waking world. Lakes and rivers passed, and sometimes a zinc roof in a jungle settlement caught the sun rays and sent a jittery flash of light up to him. The world spread out like water without containment. Looking at the horizon, he discovered it was not really there at all, but the line between sky and earth was altogether lost in an aerial haze much thicker than the mists of morning. He was seeing the entire waking world, just as he had seen the entire Dream World when last he'd been in the Big Fish's belly, and both went on forever.

He knew now that the waking and dreaming worlds had come together within him, sealing both worlds in his soul. Dreaming and waking were one. That was the deep secret of the Big Fish. The waking world was as huge and mysterious as the dreaming world. So the Iban had been right all along when they claimed this was so. It was not merely the talk of old people in the longhouse and of dayungs in meditation rooms. He was witnessing the truth of it in a way no Iban had done before. The Big Fish was showing him the deepest of secrets as it swam on with a roar through the depths of the sky.

"Bayang?"

He turned to stare at Harry's puzzled face.

"Why smiling? So happy?" Harry asked in Iban.

Bayang told him what he couldn't understand. "I am seeing the world through the eyes of the Big Fish."

What Harry did understand, however, was his friend's obvious joy. Together they stood at the cockpit window and peered out at the rain forests of Borneo, at the rumpled clouds passing by, and the zigzag threads of river conforming to the shape of gullied hills in the massed greenery.

"Good," Harry said, pointing at the swiftly moving miles of forest below.

Bayang wondered if all white men were like his friend, who could say only one word to describe a world as vast as the realm of spirits. But what really mattered was wai—the friend himself—and Bayang would be forever grateful to Harry for getting him into the belly of the Big Fish. His deepest gratitude was reserved for Duck Foot, who had seen the sign, who had understood the long wait was over, who had led him to his destiny.

·18·

"So they're home by now," Officer Windsor said to his nephew as they sat on the veranda.

"They must be. They went by launch all the way to Kapit. From there it's a week by dugout."

"I don't imagine they thanked you for what you did for them."

"No, they said nothing."

Uncle Julian nodded sagely. "There's no 'thank you' in the Iban language. They don't expect acknowledgment for an act of kindness. To them it's natural to be either kind—or cruel."

"I like that. I didn't thank them for what they did for me either."

"Is there anything you don't like about the Iban?"

"I don't like one of their special treats—river fish boiled with sour fruit."

"I won't ask if you miss your friends. That's obvious enough. But I suppose you'll have plenty in your own life to deal with soon."

He was referring to Harry's return to England for the winter term of school.

"Rajah Brooke asked me about them yesterday," continued Uncle Julian. "They've made quite a stir in the colony here. It's a shame he never met them."

"I'm glad he didn't."

"Why is that?"

"Rajah Buk would have seen a girl who no longer limped thanks to British kindness. And a boy who was given the ride of his life in an airplane. He'd have patted them on the head and sent them away."

"Unfair, nephew. I hope your experience in the jungle won't turn you into someone who has contempt for his own kind and country. I find that exceedingly unappealing."

"Contempt for my kind and country is not possible for me." Harry's determined response silenced his uncle.

They sat for a time listening to the call of a lone cuckoo in a tree—three notes ascending, then repeated and repeated in a way that many people found maddening.

"There's something I still don't understand," Uncle Julian said after a while. He was lighting his meerschaum pipe. "You say the plane ride was what the boy was searching for all along?"

"Yes, but he didn't know it."

Officer Windsor sighed. He let the subject go, though he might have made this comment: I told you the difficulty of dealing with the Dayak people. To understand them you'd have to enter their Dream World.

Uncle Julian was relieved that the Iban departure was the end of it, so he was unsettled one day when two warriors, bare chests and legs ornately tattooed, showed up at the cottage door. Abik was sent for as interpreter. They had come for Tuan Harry at the request of Pamancha Dana, headman of the longhouse south of the Rajang River junction with the Balui.

One of the men took out a pouch and removed something from it.

"Why, Harry, it's your locket!" Julian exclaimed.

Abik spoke with the Iban, then said to Harry, "Good mother to you. Good mother to us. That's the message from your friend."

"And he wants me to go back with these men?" Harry asked. Without awaiting an answer, he declared, "I will!"

"Wait a minute," Uncle Julian said. "That's a long trip coming and going. You have to leave for school in a month."

"Enough time," Harry claimed.

"And I suppose you don't mind being late," his uncle said with a frown.

"I'll make it up. And anyway, Bayang's sent for me. He returned the locket, which means he no longer needs it. But I'm wanted there."

"That's true," put in Abik. "He has taken the Dream Walk and knows who he is. There'll be a celebration of it and he wants his friend there."

"Then I'm going." Harry didn't turn to ask permission of his uncle. He was going.

Realizing that, Julian Windsor cleared his throat and said, "Well, get cracking. There's no time to waste."

The two Iban, Harry, and Abik (along for interpreting) took a shallow-draft launch up the Rajang River. They motored on brackish water between twin walls of scrub bush and mangrove all the way to Kapit. From this river town they traveled by a dugout that the Iban had left with friendly Melanau tribesmen who lived nearby. The river narrowed into a snaky tunnel of white water, then thinned in a sluggish brown ribbon canopied over for long stretches with thick branches and dangling moss. Sitting amidships while the Iban stroked their paddles, Harry recaptured the excitement of entering the jungle. Animals appeared at the riverbank, coming for a drink. He saw monkeys, honey bears, barking deer. Overhead in the trees there were parakeets racketing and crested jays and maroon woodpeckers. He saw the blunt snout of a river turtle that passed along the port side of the dugout. The huge webbed claws moved silently beneath the surface. As the boat glided along, he saw purple orchids growing out of rotting branches, and thickets of giant bamboo more than a hundred feet high, and he heard the wood-creaking cry of the hornbill just inland from the bank. And he had glimpses of backwater where buffalo lay with their noses exposed, the soft flesh testing the air as delicately as the antennae of insects. He heard the grunting of wild pigs in the undergrowth alongside the river. Black eagles soared overhead. Iridescent dragonflies lighted upon the sweaty muscled back of the Iban paddling in the bow.

Harry felt himself smiling, because he was here again, in the jungle. How could he leave it a second time? The sights and sounds and smells held him firmly in their grip, perhaps forever. This is where I belong, Harry told himself exultantly. But did he? That question brought a rush of sadness and confusion. Where, really, did he belong?

Two days later, after they passed the final outpost of civilization at Belaga and turned at last southward into the Balui River, it seemed to Harry as if he had never left the Bornean jungle. Kuching was no more than a dream. England was a half-forgotten memory. This was the only reality. He told that to Abik, whose only response was a smile so thin that it seemed as disapproving as a frown.

But the next morning, when a mist covered the motionless surface of the Balui, the Iban tracker, who sat in front of Harry in the dugout, turned and said, "We'll be there soon. You mustn't worry. You mustn't think too much. You must enjoy yourself and feel good about your friends."

Before Harry even saw the longhouse, he heard its welcome—a Malay blunderbuss was fired into the air and its booming noise had birds flapping wildly out of trees like debris blown outward from an explosion. As the dugout approached a sharp bend in the river, a young Iban onshore raised a brace of wood partridge and his blowgun high in greeting. Then the boat came around in full view of the longhouse. Rising on long stilts parallel to the muddy bank, its hardwood shingles glistening in the sunlight, the long building commanded an entire hill. All along the veranda people were staring down at the boat. They had known of its approach for a long time.

Soon after dawn Bayang had been awakened by his mother, who told him that the dugout was no more than an hour downstream. "Your friend has come," she said with a smile.

He was on the veranda with the crowd when Harry climbed the muddy bank and shinnied up the grease-slick log with arms and legs wrapped cautiously around it, so that people tittered and finally laughed. Harry did, too, when he reached the longhouse floor, and the two boys embraced.

"Where's Duck Foot?" he asked immediately.

"I'll tell you about her." Bayang led him along the passageway lined with curious Iban until coming to his family's room. His mother did not acknowledge the visitor's presence, following Iban etiquette, but placed bowls of salt fish, curried buffalo, glutinous rice, and boiled yams in front of him, as the boys sat beneath a smoke-blackened rafter from which the head basket hung, having been taken in from the veranda for the celebration.

Bayang explained that Duck Foot was having her first tattoos made, so she must stay in seclusion every day and fast until nightfall. Ordinarily, in this longhouse, both arms of a girl would carry the design of a dragon with two heads or of two dragons sharing one head, but Duck Foot had broken with tradition by drawing the pattern herself. "You will see," Bayang told his friend with a smile.

"Is it very painful?" Harry asked.

Bayang described how the inky mixture of lacquer-tree soot and sugarcane juice was punched into the skin. The flesh was struck by a hammer equipped with two sharp needles. "Very painful," Bayang admitted with a grimace.

"But Duck Foot won't cry."

"No, not Duck Foot."

At sunset, after Bayang had taken his friend on a tour of the longhouse, they returned to the family room, where Harry met Pamancha Dana, headman and Bayang's father, a solemn laconic man in leopard skin and hornbill feathers. And then Duck Foot arrived. Unhealed welts covered her arms. Rubbing them with sugar water had turned the welts a deep blue. The women of the longhouse had been scandalized when she had drawn this shape and insisted on using it as the chief design for both arms. In its crude way it seemed like a bird flying. But along with wings and tail, this bird had two crossed lines athwart its beak. The addition of this stylized propeller made her drawing something unbirdlike, strange, and even threatening to the women who squatted around and watched disapprovingly as it was hammered into her bloody flesh. Duck Foot sustained a thin smile throughout the tattooing. It would take four years for all of the work to be completed on hands, arms, and legs. Some of the tattoos might become infected and cause fever. None of that mattered. She was going to carry the look of a Vickers Vimy on her flesh for the rest of her life.

A huge fire on the riverbank signaled the beginning of the celebration. Women wore clinking roundels of beaten silver on loops of rattan around their necks. Warriors polished their parangs and for the occasion were allowed to wear hornbill feathers in their hair, just like the headman. Mounds of food were distributed on banana fronds to everyone assembled from the longhouse.

Although his wai sat next to him, Bayang soon forgot Harry's presence and that of Duck Foot and of everyone except his father. After the huge feast, Bayang rose to tell of his Dream Walk. It was to Pamancha Dana that he addressed his words.

He described the Big Fish who urged him to see the world as it is by taking the Dream Walk. In detail he acknowledged the loyalty and help of Duck Foot, the generosity of his white friend, and claimed that the Dream Walk would have failed had they not been with him. He spoke finally of the end of the Dream Walk, when dreaming and waking became one and the same in the Big Fish's belly. "What our ancestors told us was true is true. The world's as big as our dream of it. In the belly of the Big Fish, looking through its eyes, I saw the world as a place without end, with land below and sky above. The Iban have always been right: what our eyes and our dreams tell us are both true. This is what the Dream Walk taught me. I have seen how big the waking world is, and how small, even as small as the dreaming space in a man's head. I don't fear what I now know. The world beyond our longhouse may go on forever, but it's not as deep into the heart as our world here. I am proud, Father, of our life."

Next morning Harry was nudged awake and looked up to see the copper-colored, unsmiling face of Bayang. Behind the young warrior stood Duck Foot, who was out of seclusion now that the first round of tattooing had been completed. Harry got up and followed them down the passageway and the ladder into a clearing. Abik waited for them there. Nearby were cages where chickens stayed for the night, so that Pebnako, the unseen winged beast, might not get them.

"Your friends want to say something," Abik explained.

They waited while Duck Foot released and fed the chickens,

then while she unpenned some pigs that scooted for a mud-hole and debris under the longhouse floor.

"Last night," Bayang said to Harry through Abik, "you told us you wanted to stay here."

"I do," Harry acknowledged. He had sworn to stay forever. "I think I belong here. It'll be my home, too, if you'll have me."

Bayang shook his head. "No. Please go back now. Today. This morning."

When Abik translated these words, he added, "Your friend doesn't mean to be rude."

"But—he's throwing me out!"

"Your friend stays here for the rest of his life. He'll be the headman someday. You must go back where you came from and be what you should be. Your friend has found out who he is. Now you must do the same."

Later that morning, when the dugout was ready at the shore-line, the entire longhouse turned out to see the departure.

Harry said to Bayang, "You're right, I suppose. There's no place for me here."

The young Iban touched the chain around Harry's neck, lifted the locket with thumb and forefinger, and looked hard at it. "Good mother to us. Good mother to you."

"Yes, good mother to all of us," Harry said.

"My father thanks you for coming. And I do and Duck Foot and our people. It would not have been the Dream Walk without you."

Looking at the young warrior and the tattooed girl, Harry could think of nothing to say. For an instant he was deep in the jungle with them, eating wild pig.

Abik and two boatmen waited for him at the riverbank. Getting into the dugout, Harry sat up straight and didn't turn to glance over his shoulder at the first bend of the river, so that he lost a final look at the longhouse and his friends, waving from the muddy shore.

The rhythmic paddling went on for hours, while Harry stared at the passing undergrowth and towering trees and animals coming down for a drink. Within a few days Harry began seeing another world: motor launches, zinc roofs on two-story buildings, riverside markets with gramophones and sewing machines to sell. Soon he'd have a glimpse of cottages in the hills of Kuching, hear ships' whistles blowing, and later the groan of windlasses on decks loaded with cargo from all over the world.

He felt a quickening of his pulse, as the future lay far, far beyond the Rajang River. His friends were right. The greatest proof of their friendship had been to send him away. It was time to go on.